THEN & NOW®

YONKERS

Opposite: Getty Square, named after Robert Parkhill Getty, is the city's original hub. Today "the square" is Yonkers's mass transit focal point and home to many of the city's historic buildings. This photograph is of the No. 2 trolley on Palisade Avenue heading toward Getty Square in the 1920s. Electric trolleys replaced horsecars in 1892 and, on November 12, 1952, Yonkers had its last trolley ride. (Courtesy of Yonkers Historical Society.)

THEN & NOW®

YONKERS

Yonkers Historical Society and
the Blue Door Artist Association

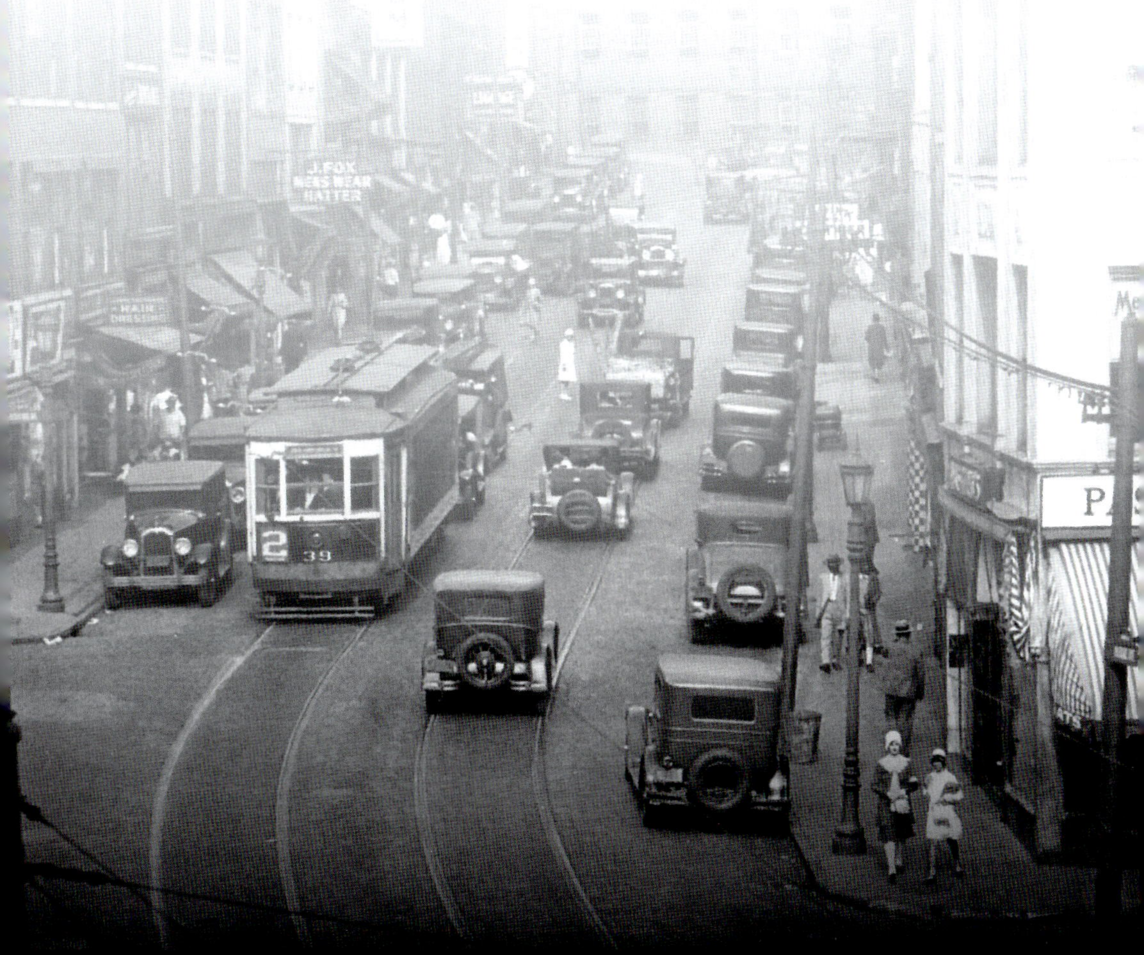

ISBN 978-0-7385-5760-1

Library of Congress control number: 2007935334

Published by Arcadia Publishing
Charleston, South Carolina

Printed in the United States of America

For all general information contact Arcadia Publishing at:
Telephone 843-853-2070
Fax 843-853-0044
E-mail sales@arcadiapublishing.com
For customer service and orders:
Toll-Free 1-888-313-2665

Visit us on the Internet at www.arcadiapublishing.com

On the front cover: Larkin Plaza, in downtown Yonkers, is located at the center of many sites key to the development of the city. For centuries the Nepperhan River attracted many to this area including the Leni Lenape Native American tribe, Adriaen Van der Donck (the man who the city of Yonkers is named after), and several generations of the Philipse family, who located their manor hall nearby. Until the late 19th century, the area was a millpond created by the damming of the Nepperhan River. In the 1920s, the river was placed in a flume below the site and the area reconfigured to provide parking for a growing downtown. Today the plaza anchors not only Philipse Manor Hall, but Yonkers train station, the Riverfront branch of the Yonkers Public Library, the city's main post office, and the city's Spanish American War monument. (Courtesy of Yonkers Historical Society.)

On the back cover: In 1876, one of the many traveling parties that used the famous trail known as South Broadway is on an outing. This photograph was taken in front of the Getty House. (Courtesy of Yonkers Historical Society.)

Contents

Acknowledgments

The Yonkers Historical Society and the Blue Door Artist Association presented their first collaborative exhibition of photographs, Yonkers: Then and Now, in 2005. The exhibit juxtaposed historic and contemporary photographs of Yonkers. The historic photographs were borrowed and scanned from numerous public and private sources, while local photographers provided contemporary images of the city to display alongside them. Because of the great interest expressed by viewers of the exhibition, we decided to publish this book. Those of us who helped put it together had one intention—to show change over time in Yonkers through the use of historic and new photographs.

What has emerged is a chronicle of a city that has changed vastly, yet not so radically that its past cannot be recognized. Yes, there are locations that would not be familiar to residents of Yonkers 100 years ago. But if you look, there are glimpses. The bend in a road, a lone smokestack, and the parapet of a building's roof are still there. To those of us who love this city and its rich history, it is pleasing to know that numerous aspects of Yonkers's built legacy are still intact. From public buildings to residential streets, parts of this city could be viewed now as though decades of time had stood still.

To the many people who gave their time or materials and to the organizations that allowed us access to their historic photographs, we are deeply grateful. The historic photographs are from the Crestwood Historical Society, Flynn Memorial Trust, Hudson River Museum, Donald Kreutzberg, Nepera Park Civic Association, Philipse Manor Hall, Hon. Nicholas Spano, Yonkers Riverfront Library, Westchester County Historical Society, Yonkers Historical Society, and former city archivist Richard Moore. The following individuals and organizations assisted with photographing the contemporary images and writing descriptions: Grace Braley, Sam Brown, Mario Caruso, Mary Fennel, Rosalie Flynn, Frank Furrelle, Ralph Gabriner, Ned Harris, Joan Jennings, Toby McAfee, Elizabeth McFadden, Martin McGloin, David Nieves, Luis Perelman, Turhan Von Brandon, Jonathan Wallen, Mimi Welsh, Jeffrey Williams, Madeline Wilson, Marianne and Len Winstanley, the Yonkers Department of Public Works, and the Yonkers Fire Department. Thanks also to John Favareau and Steve Force of the Yonkers Public Library. Sources for the text of this book include the Yonkers Historical bulletins, volumes 1 through 30, 1953–1984; the Yonkers Historical Society newsletters, the *Yonkers Historian*; and archives of the Yonkers Historical Society.

The assembly and coordination of the photographs and text that comprise this book were only possible due to the extraordinary efforts of Luis Perelman and Marianne Winstanley. Their commitment to this endeavour reflects the spirit of Yonkers and its people.

Jeffrey Williams, President
Yonkers Historical Society

Introduction

Founded in 1646 by Adriaen Van Der Donck, whose title *Jonkheer* (Dutch for "young gentleman"), became the city's name, Yonkers served as the administrative center for the vast Philipse estate until the American Revolution. Incorporated as a village in 1855 and a city in 1872, Yonkers is a beautiful river town sitting on the scenic Hudson River opposite the towering Palisades. From pre-Revolutionary times through the American Revolution, the Industrial Revolution, the Gilded Age, and the 20th century, Yonkers has maintained its small-town flavor. Getty Square, once the city's hub and the focal point of its mass transportation, is still home to many historic buildings. As a leading industrial center located on the river, Yonkers was the place where Elisha Graves Otis and sons manufactured the safety elevator, where Edwin Armstrong first demonstrated FM radio transmission, where Leo Baekeland invented Bakelite, and where Charles Harvey engineered the first elevated train. The fourth largest city in the state of New York and known for its many fine neighborhoods, Yonkers is home to golf in America (1888), the second oldest annual marathon in the country, the Cross County Center, and many cultural institutions. Development is now spreading throughout the city as Yonkers enters a new phase of its history.

The Yonkers Historical Society first began in 1882 as "the Committee on the Historical Records of Yonkers." In 1895, the society helped to preserve historic Philipse Manor Hall when there was a move to demolish it. When the historic Sherwood House (1740) was threatened with destruction in the early 1950s, a small group of dedicated citizens succeeded in saving and preserving it. The group also assumed the records of the Yonkers branch of the Westchester Historical Society and formed the Yonkers Historical Society as it is known today. Chartered by the New York State Board of Regents of the New York State Education Department, the Yonkers Historical Society strives to preserve the historic records, structures, and sites of the city, in the hope of saving Yonkers's rich heritage for future generations.

The Blue Door Artist Association, founded in 2002, is a not-for-profit organization dedicated to bringing art to local communities throughout the tristate area that are currently underserved by art programs and exhibitions. The association creates and organizes exhibitions, public art projects, workshops, and special events.

Every effort has been made to insure the historical accuracy of the materials presented in *Yonkers*. However, the authors welcome any comments regarding the book and its contents.

CHAPTER

DOWNTOWN YONKERS

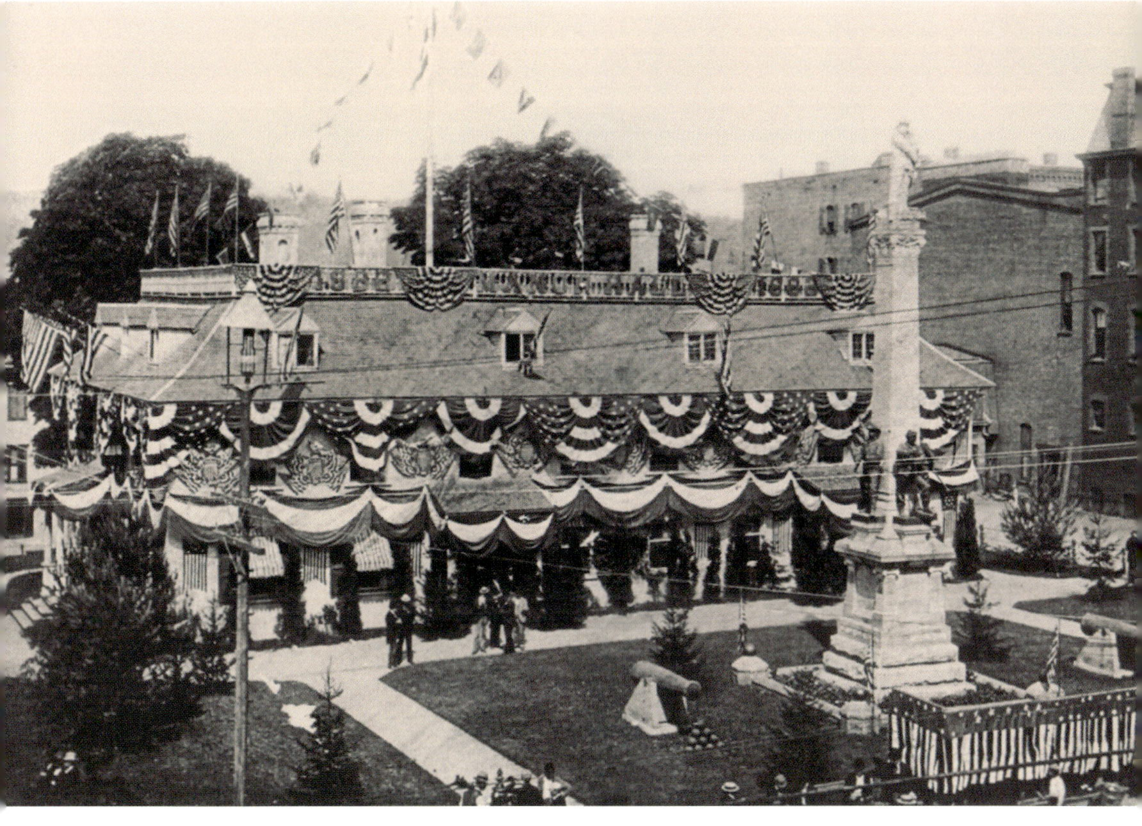

In 1882, Philipse Manor celebrated its 200th anniversary. It is the oldest house in southern Westchester County and is the house around which Yonkers grew and developed. Today it offers holiday and ethnic celebrations, special tours and programs, musical performances, and children's programs. The Soldiers and Sailors Monument was erected in 1891 and 1892. (Courtesy of Yonkers Historical Society.)

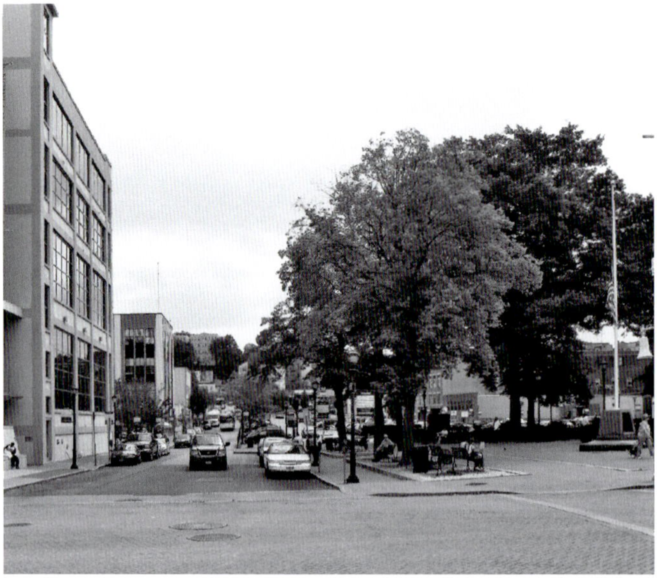

Larkin Plaza, located between Warburton Avenue and River Street, bears little resemblance to "the wedge" of the 1920s. Late in the 1920s, the last stretch of the Saw Mill River was put into a flume and covered. Named for Mayor Thomas Larkin, the plaza was constructed on top of the flume. Few buildings survived the wrecking ball. One that did is the former Otis Elevator building on the corner. Completely renovated, it houses the main branch of the public library. (Courtesy of Yonkers Historical Society.)

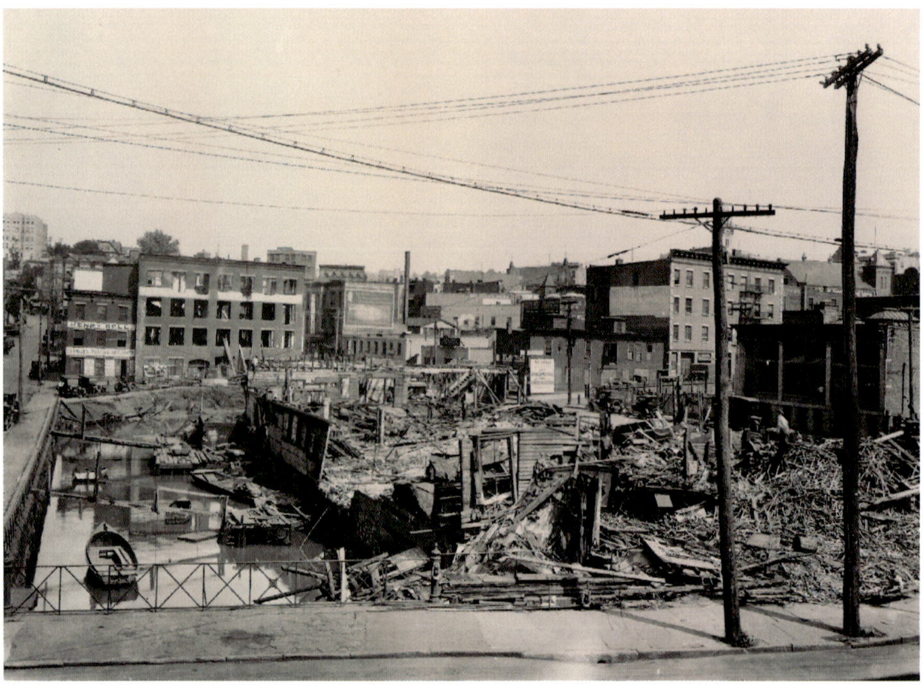

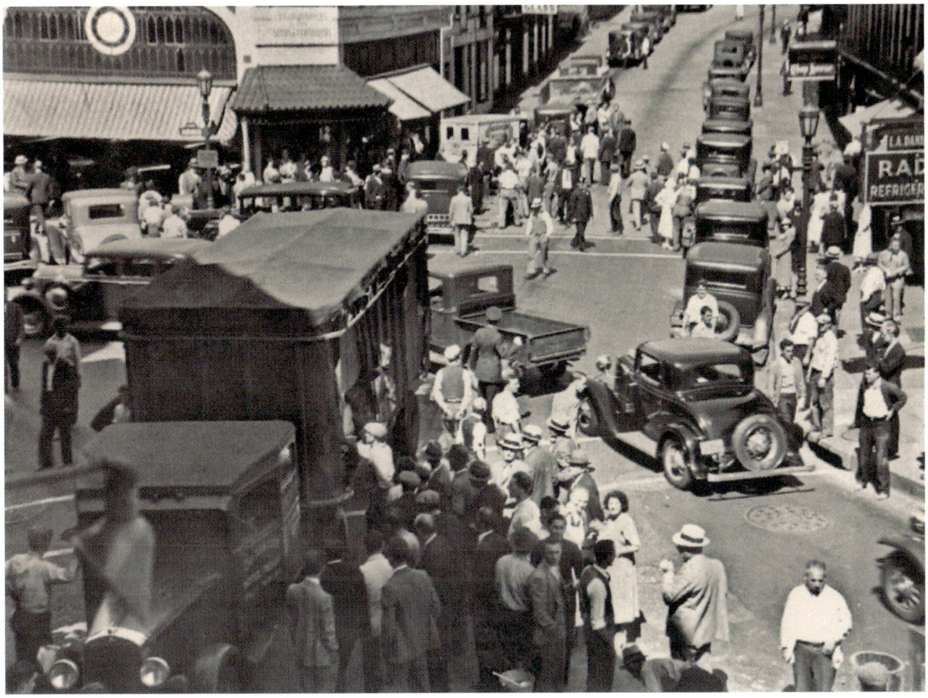

Manor House Square is located between Warburton Avenue and U.S. Route 9, the original Albany Post Road, and takes its name from the nearby Philipse Manor Hall. It is the approximate location of the waterfall that powered the gristmill built in the 1620s by Yonkers eponym, Adriaen Van Der Donck. Dating from 1857, 9 Manor House Square served as the first police headquarters and was once owned by Valentino Melah, chief steward of the White House during Pres. Ulysses S. Grant's administration. (Courtesy of Yonkers Historical Society.)

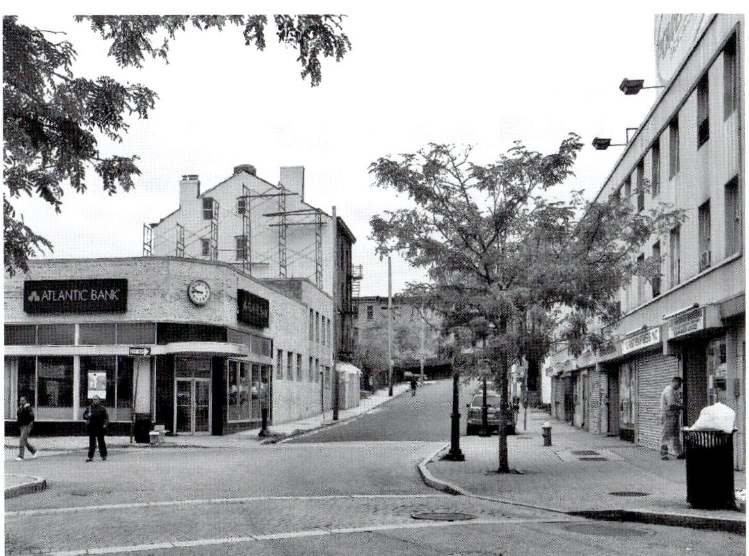

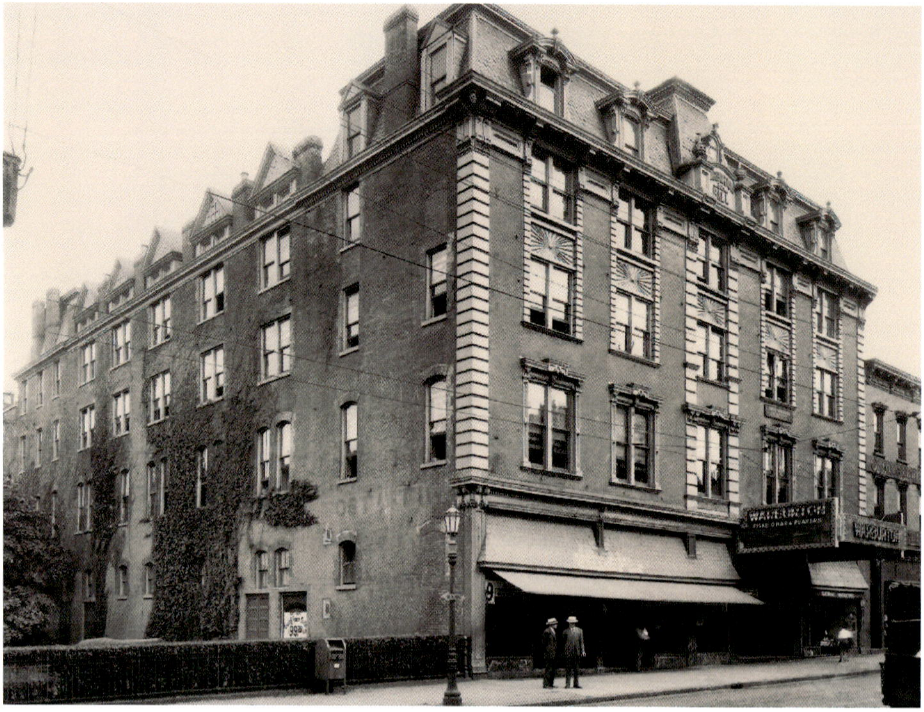

The Music Hall, located at 45 Warburton Avenue, opened formally on April 14, 1884. Henrietta Beebe, the Yonkers Glee Club, and the St. Cecilia String Quartet were among the performers on that occasion. A venue for countless musical performances and plays, the hall (later known as the Warburton Theater) was also home to high school commencements and Memorial Day exercises. The building continued in use for years after being abandoned as a theater. It was demolished in the 1970s. (Courtesy of Yonkers Historical Society.)

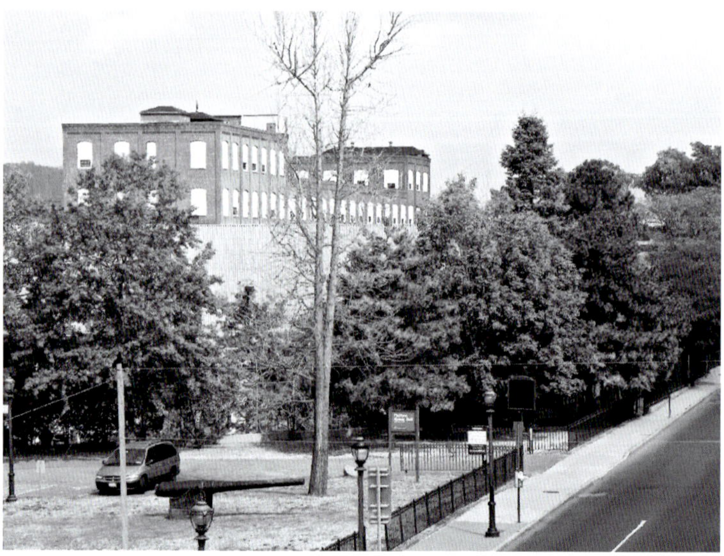

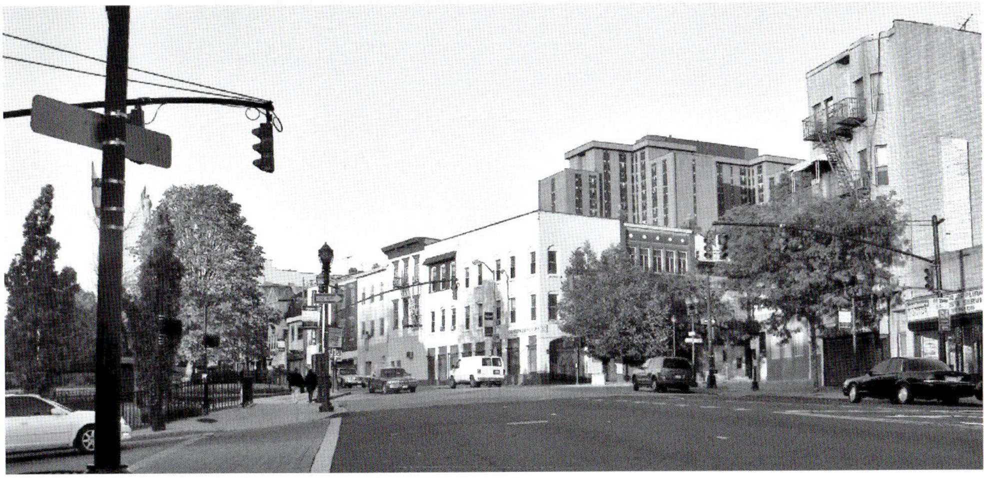

One of the longest streets in Yonkers, Warburton Avenue runs north from Getty Square into the village of Hastings. With the inauguration of the trolley (horse drawn before becoming electrified), it became possible for well-to-do Yonkers businessmen to make their homes well north of the commercial center in Getty Square. Thus Warburton Avenue became, along much of its length, a street of elegant, even stately, houses. A number of them remain to this day. (Courtesy of Yonkers Planning Bureau.)

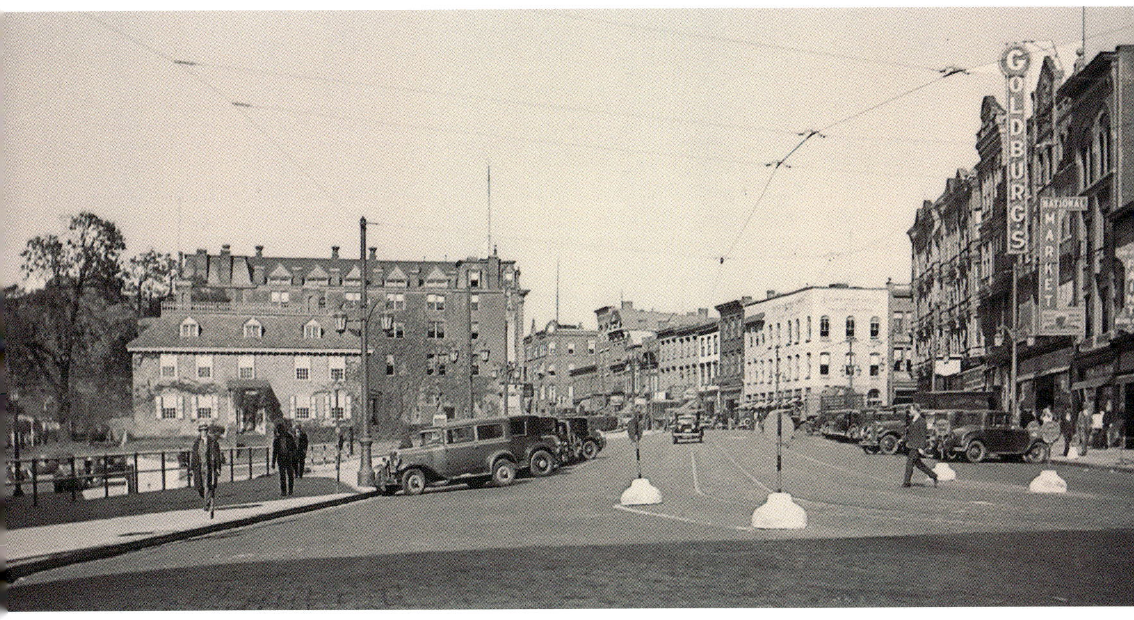

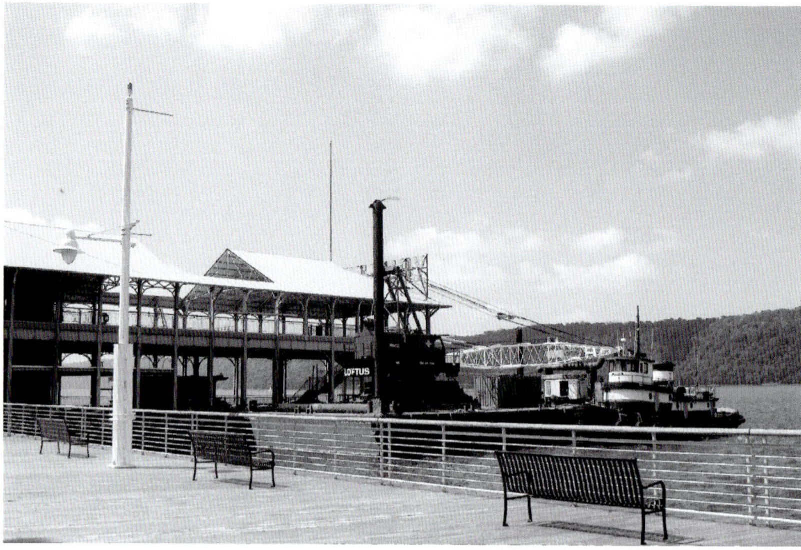

The Yonkers Recreation Pier was built for the use of the people of Yonkers around the year 1901. The Hudson River Day Liners used to stop here regularly to take passengers up the river to Bear Mountain or down the river to Rockaway. The pier was renovated in the mid-1990s. Although its roof was modified recently in order to accommodate a restaurant on the upper deck, the pier was designated a local landmark in 2007. (Courtesy of Yonkers Historical Society.)

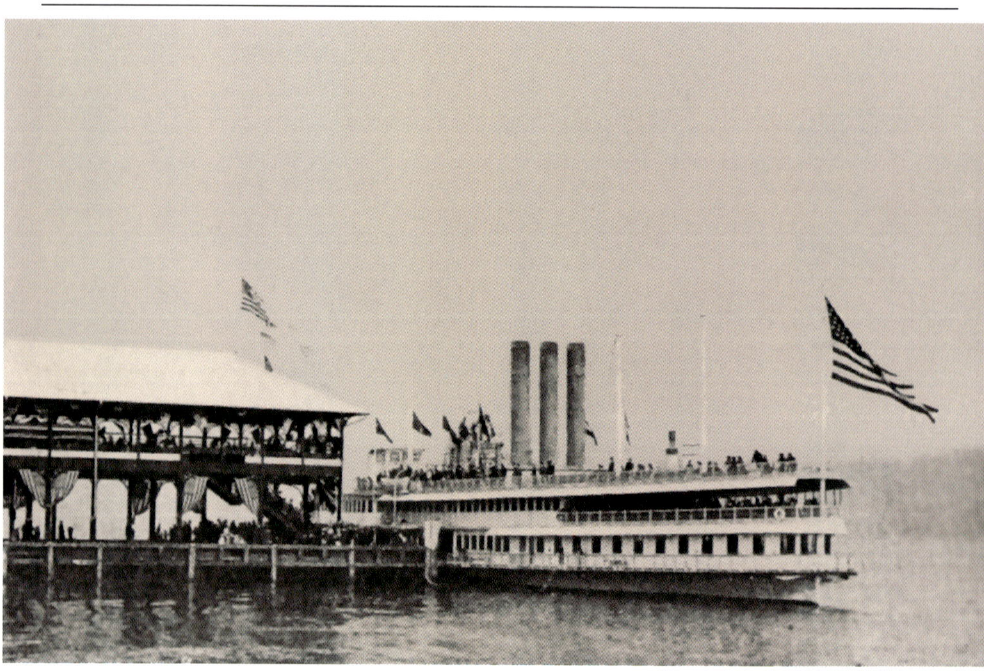

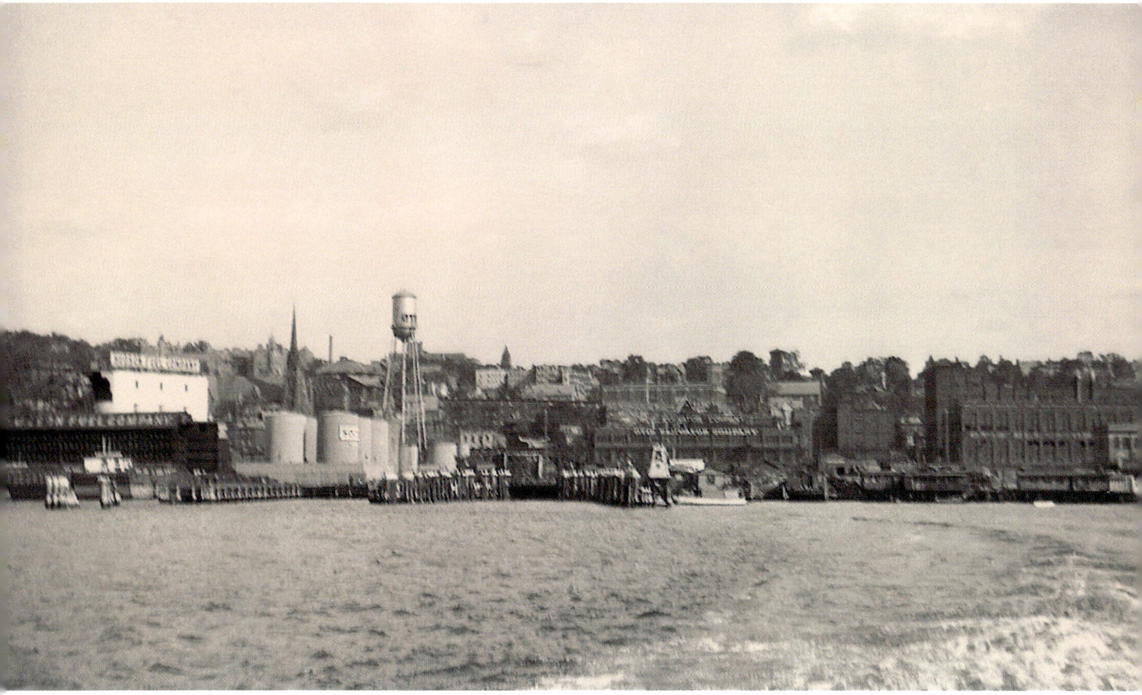

The Yonkers waterfront has played a major role in the life of the city from the time when the Hudson River provided the most accessible commercial route to and from New York City. Ferries operated between Yonkers and New Jersey for well over 100 years. The most recent, the Alpine Ferry, leaving from a dock on Alexander Street, made dozens of crossings each day until going out of business in late 1956. A Yonkers–Manhattan ferry was inaugurated in 2007. (Courtesy of Yonkers Planning Bureau.)

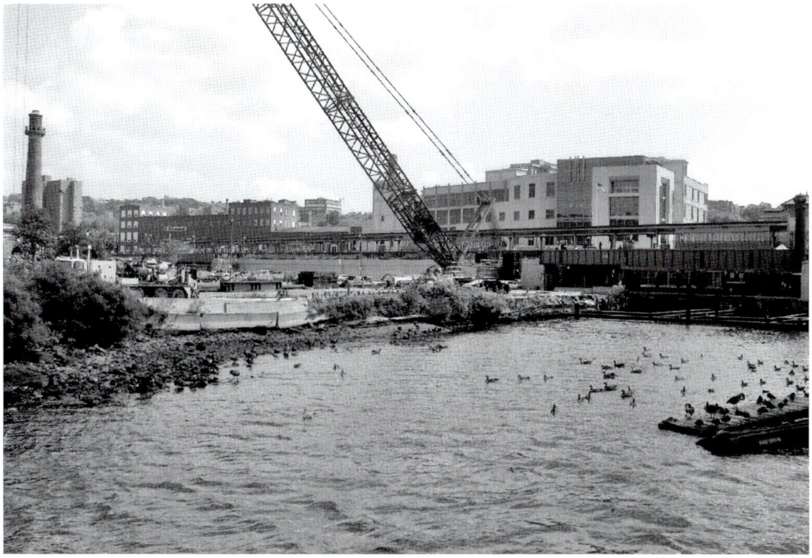

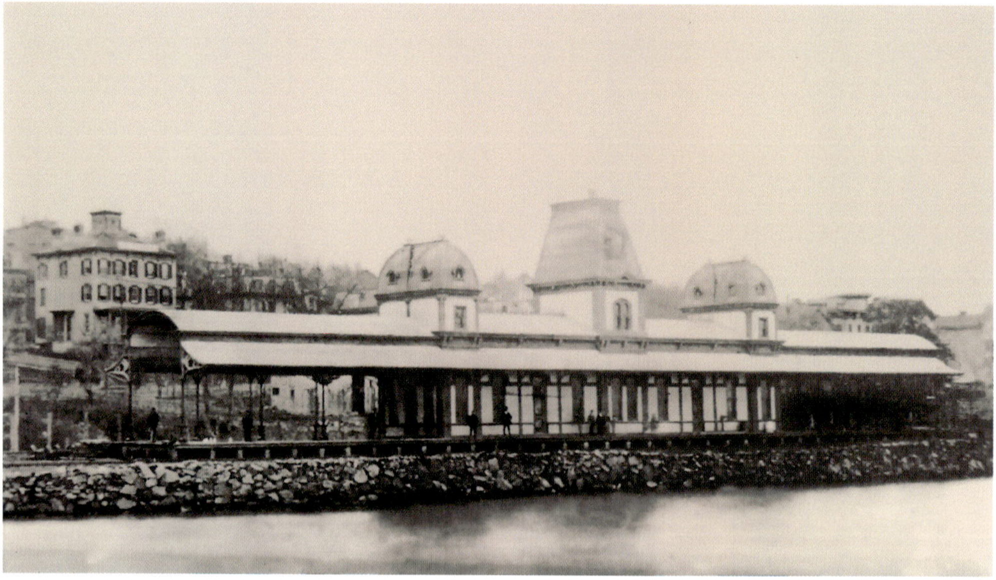

The New York Central Railroad began operation as a single-track line in 1849. For many years, the New York Central Railroad maintained a station at the foot of Ashburton Avenue, one of Yonkers's few east–west thoroughfares. The Ashburton Avenue station no longer exists. Consequently, northbound passengers who do not exit the Metro North train at the Yonkers station in Larkin Plaza must continue beyond Ashburton Avenue to the stop at the foot of Glenwood Avenue. (Courtesy of Yonkers Historical Society.)

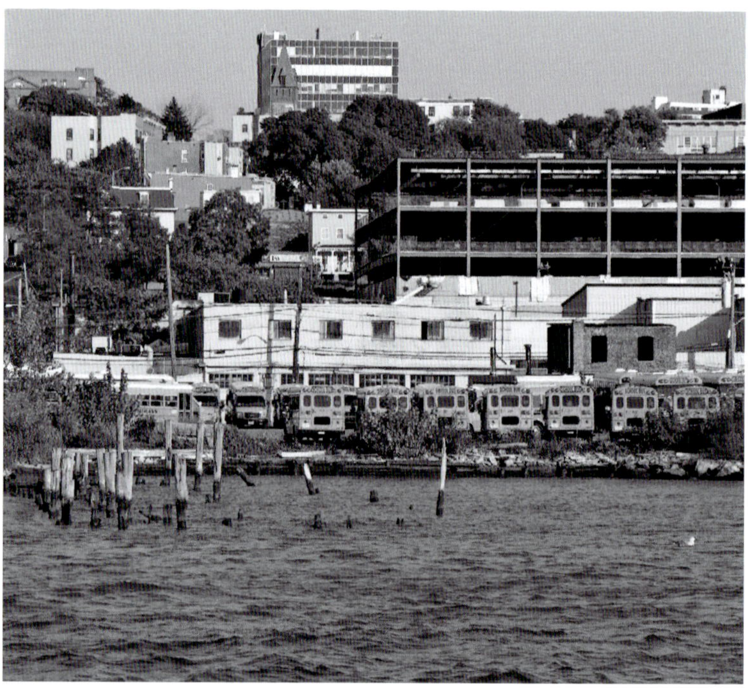

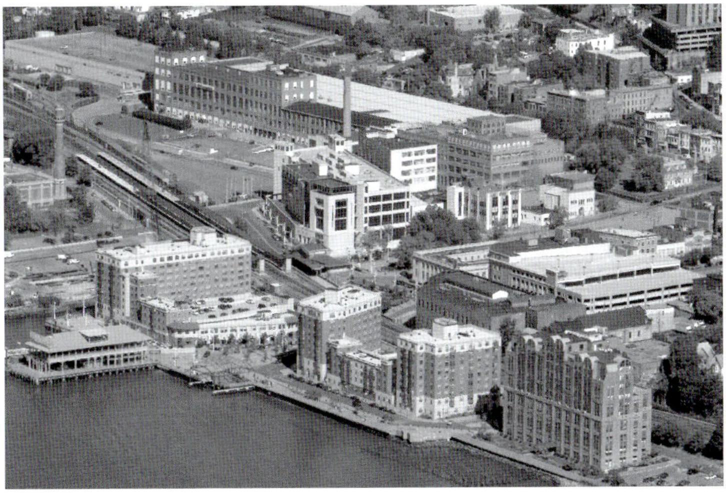

In 1853, Elisha Graves Otis invented a hoist with an automatic safety device that prevented the platform from falling if the supporting cables broke. This invention, the safety hoist, became the basis for the first safe passenger elevator, and the Otis Elevator Works became one of the largest factories in the eastern United States (seen here from the air). Acquired by United Technologies in 1976, the Otis Elevator Company vacated its Yonkers factory in 1983. (Courtesy of Hudson River Museum.)

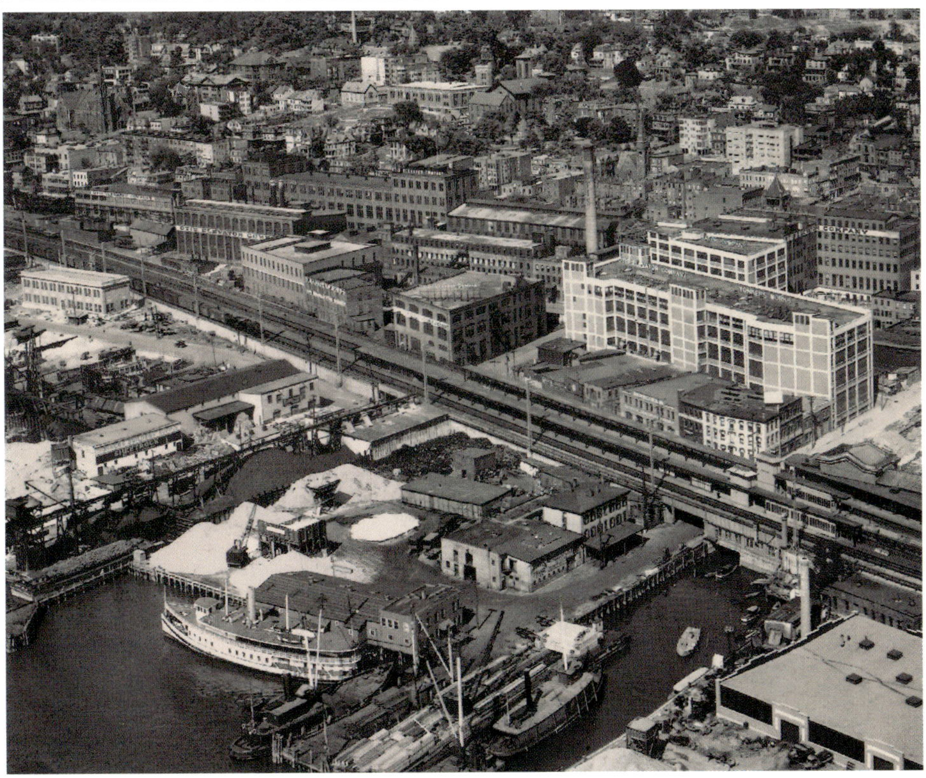

Charles P. Ward and Son, Jewelers and Opticians, was located at 23 Main Street. The Ward Clock, just outside the store, was a mainstay in Getty Square in the days when it was the central shopping area in Yonkers. Passersby would set their wristwatches by it, and shoppers could tell by glancing at it how much shopping time remained before the arrival of the next trolley. (Courtesy of Hudson River Museum.)

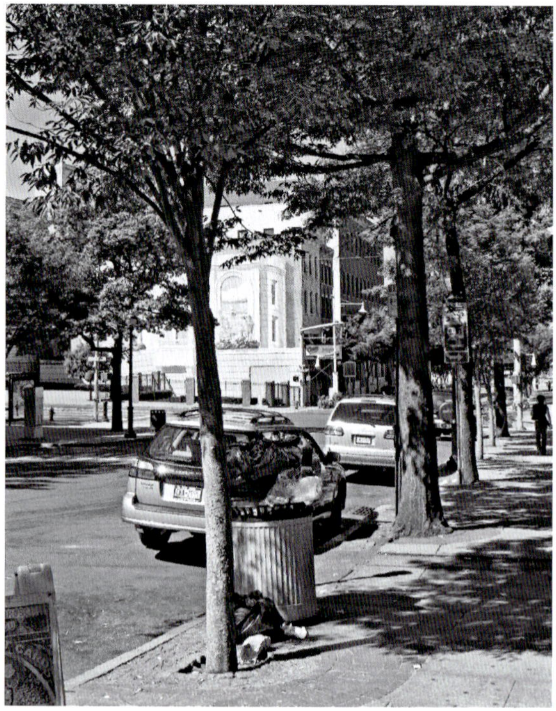

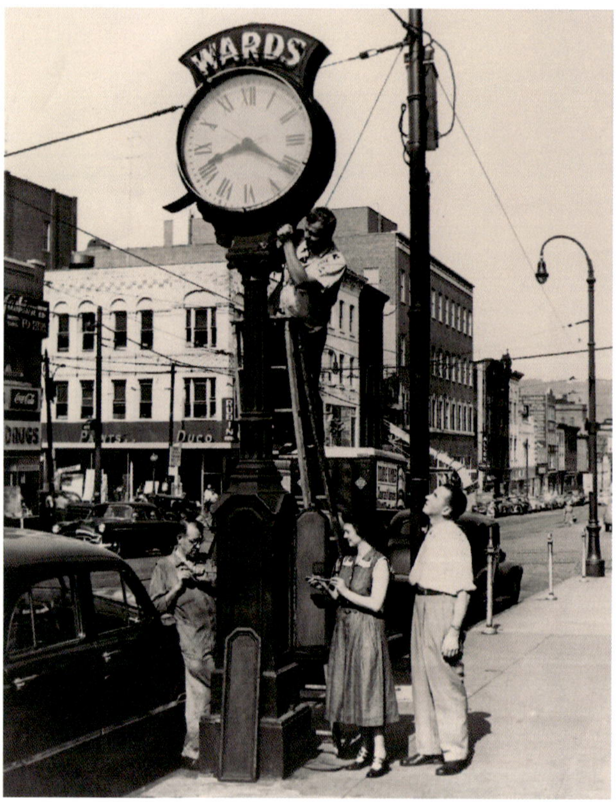

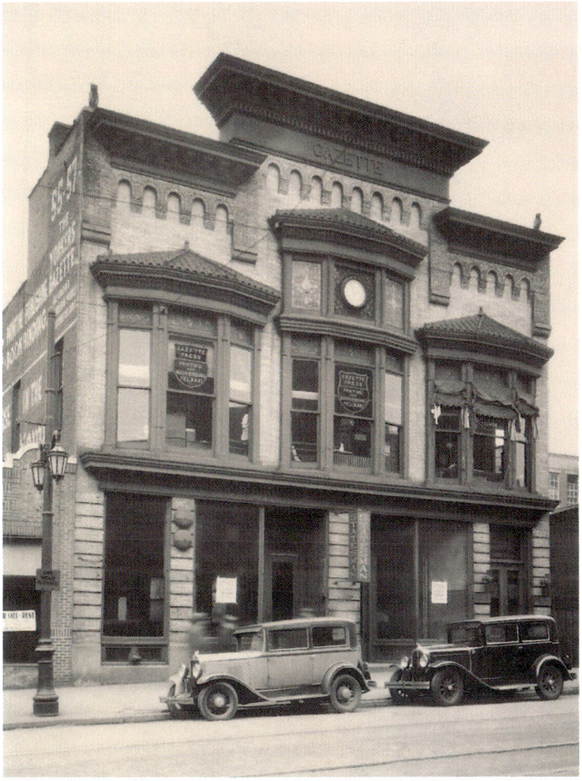

Located at 55–57 Main Street, this building was once the home of the *Yonkers Gazette*, a weekly newspaper launched in 1864 when the Yonkers Democratic Publishing Association bought out an earlier newspaper and changed the name. A merger in 1896 with Meadows Brothers Press led to the establishment of the Gazette Press at the site. The *Yonkers Gazette* ceased publication in the 1920s and Gazette Press concentrated on its printing business. Rehabilitated by the city in the late 1990s, the Gazette Building now houses a restaurant. (Courtesy of Yonkers Historical Society.)

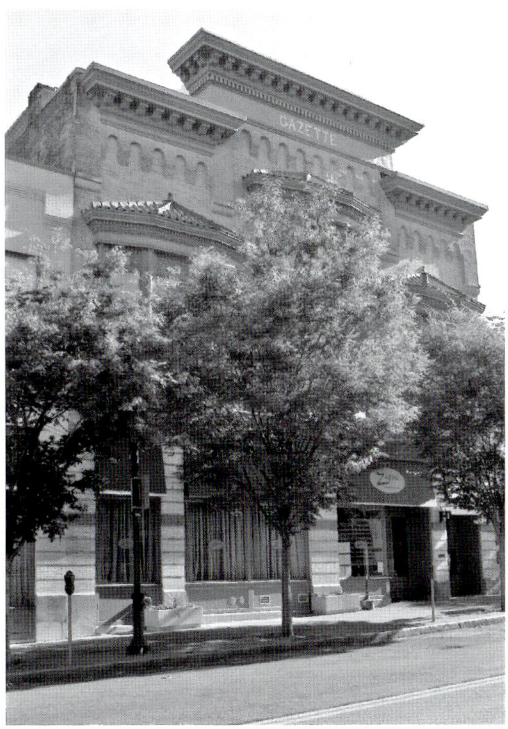

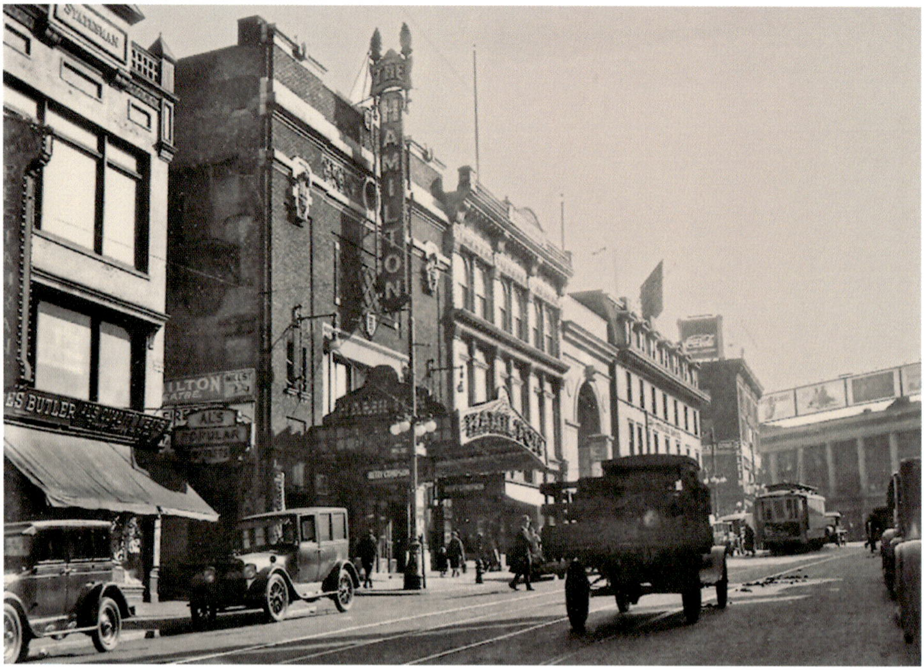

On February 29, 1913, the Hamilton Theatre opened its doors to the public at 9 Main Street. The seating capacity of the theater was about 1,000. George T. Kelly was the builder and Edwin A. Quick and Son was the architect. The building was demolished in 1927. (Courtesy of Yonkers Historical Society.)

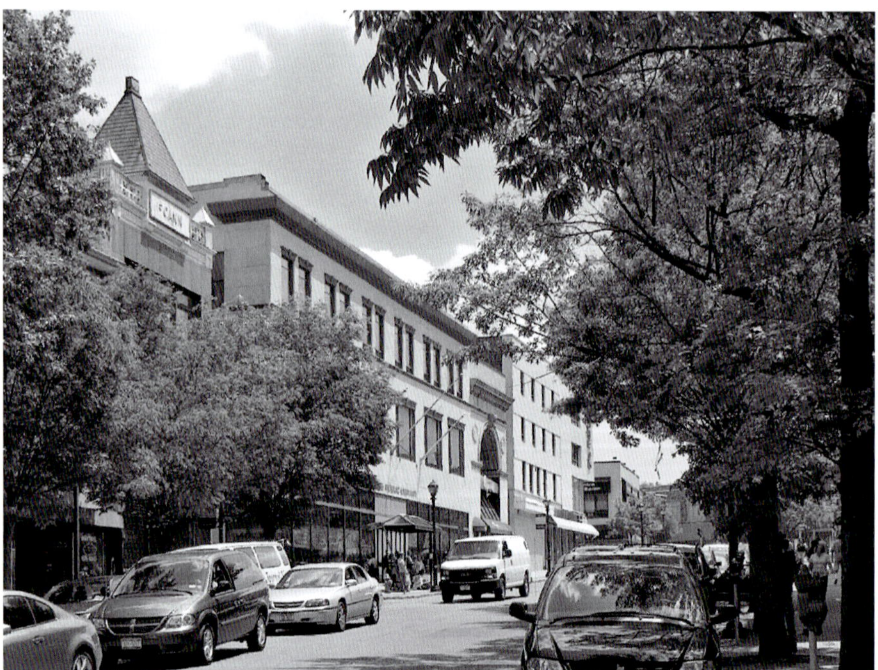

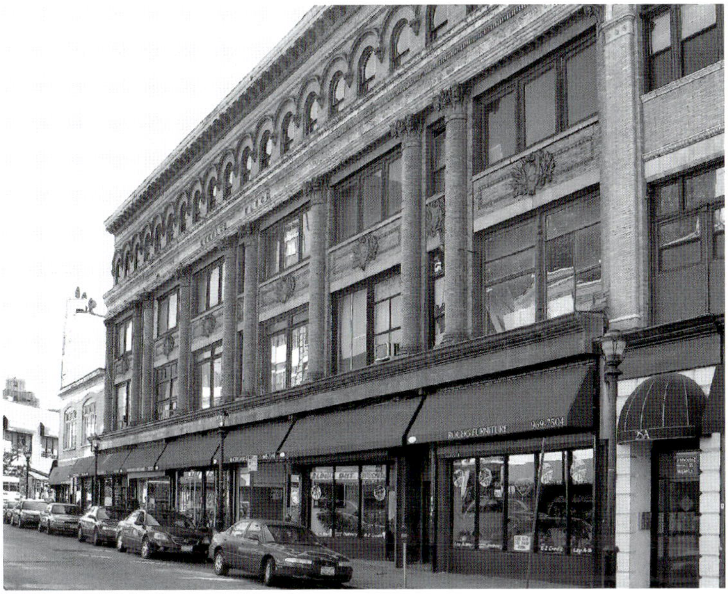

Built over the underground flume that carries the Nepperhan River, the Wheeler Block building was designed by its owner and architect, Charles Wheeler, in 1896. It consists of three separate buildings united by a common theme. Wheeler gave each of his two children one of the buildings. Monogrammed shields set above the second story identify each building's owner. (Courtesy of Yonkers Historical Society.)

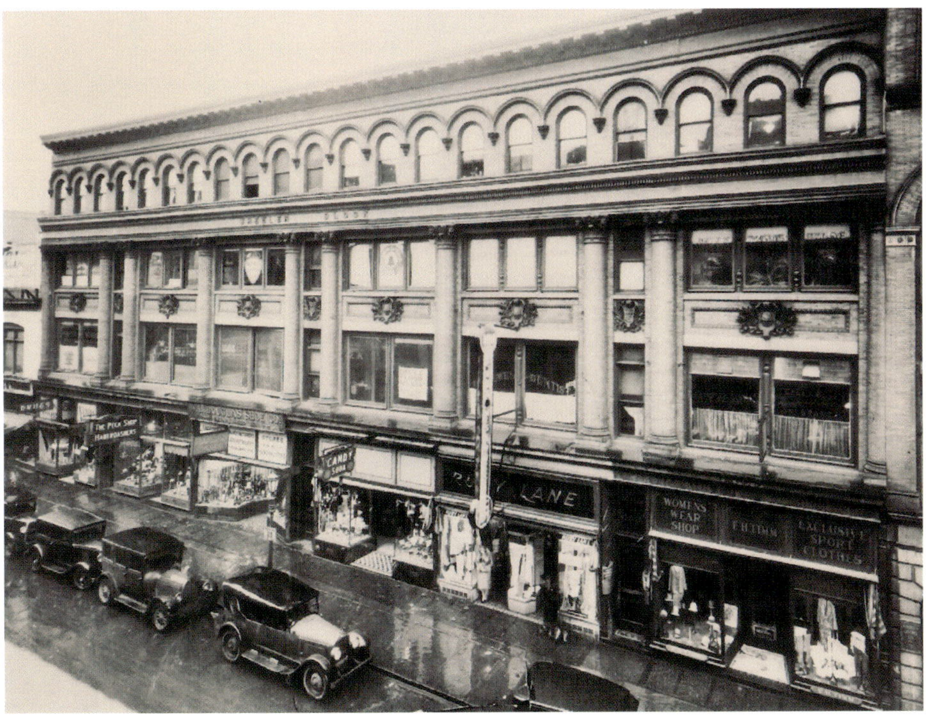

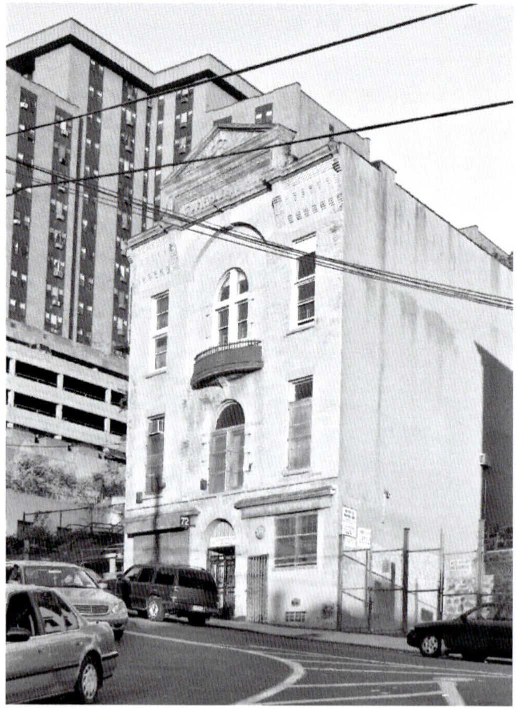

The Odd Fellows hall, located at 72–74 North Broadway, was a meeting place for members of the Independent Order of Odd Fellows, one of Yonkers's oldest fraternal organizations dedicated to caring for the widowed, the orphaned, and the needy. The hall was sold in 1946 and is now a small factory. (Courtesy of Yonkers Historical Society.)

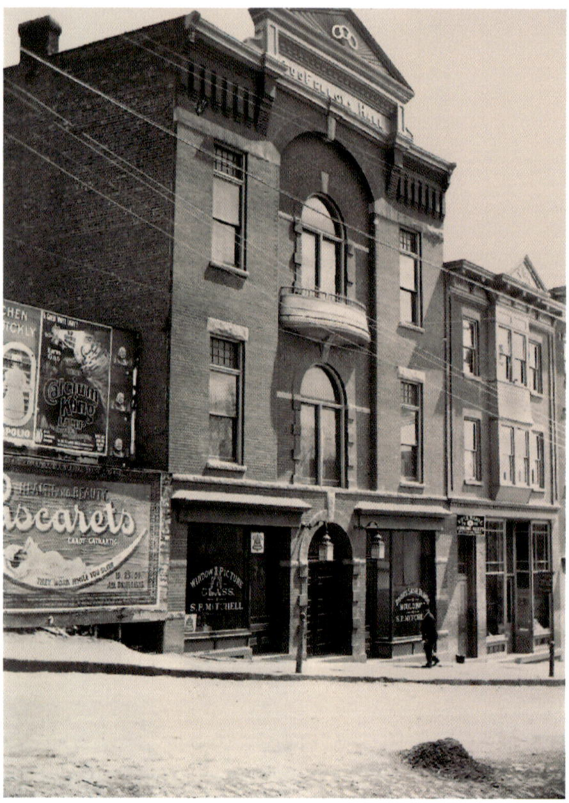

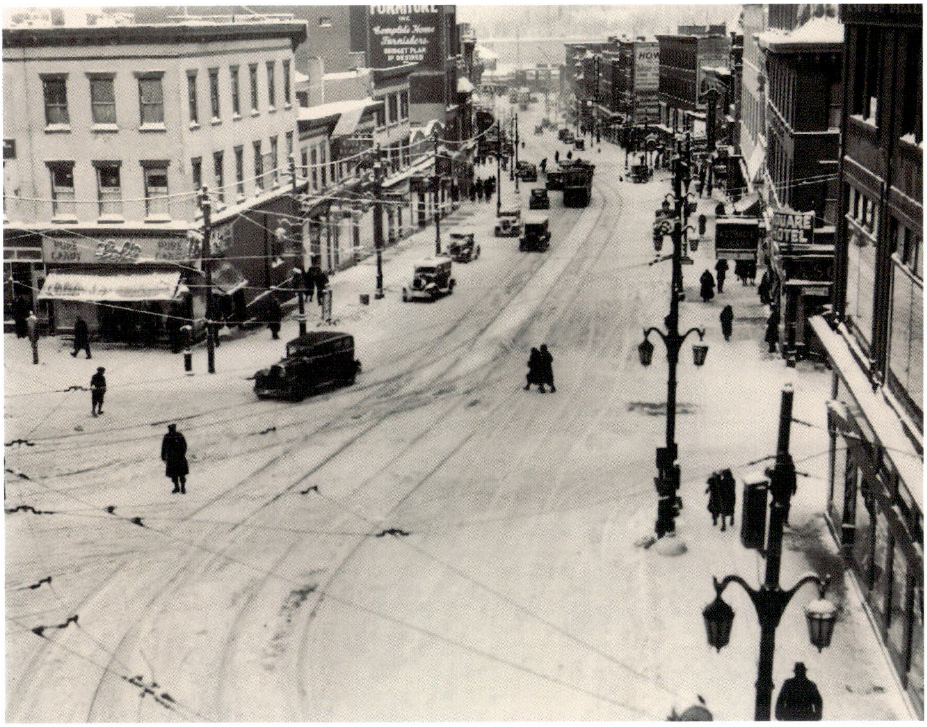

Downtown Yonkers has played a vital role in the city's evolution from a small Native American village to the fourth-largest city in New York State. Its location at the juncture of two important transportation corridors—the Hudson and Nepperhan Rivers—made it a focal point of settlement throughout history. In the post–Civil War era, Yonkers had firmly established itself as the largest city in Westchester County and one of New York's great industrial powers. (Courtesy of Yonkers Historical Society.)

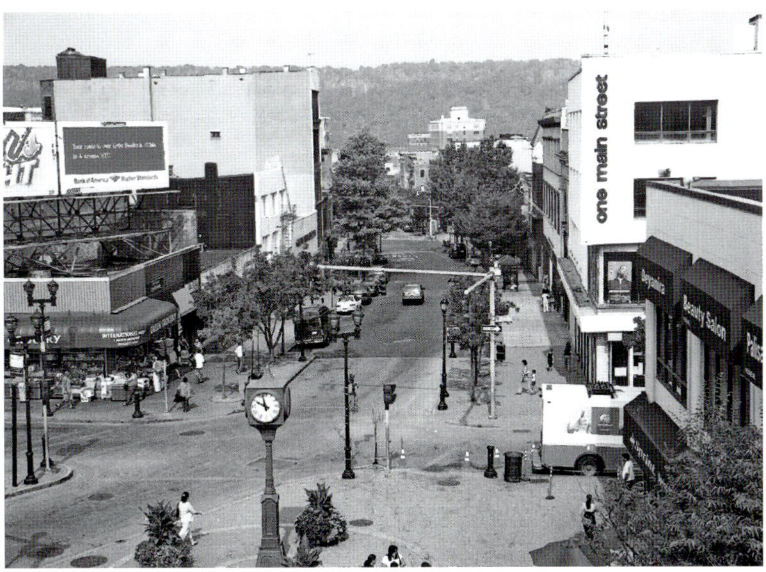

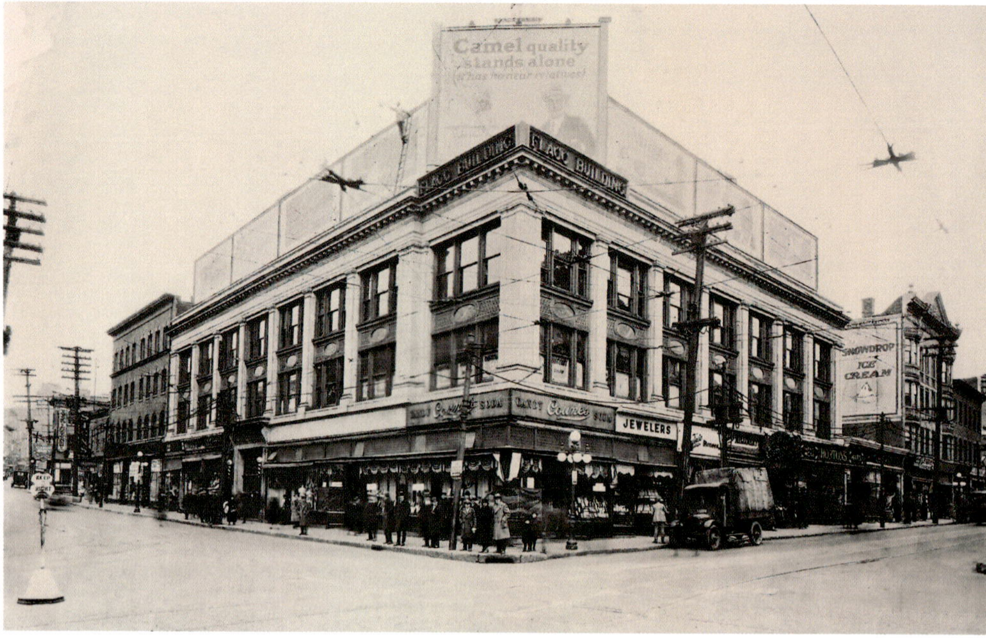

The original building on the corner of Palisade Avenue and New Main Street was erected in 1845. It was one of the first office structures erected in Yonkers that bore the name of a member of one of Yonkers's oldest families—Ethan Flagg. This building was demolished in 1915 and replaced by the Grant Company to make way for the new Grant department store. C. H. Martin department store presently occupies the site. (Courtesy of Yonkers Historical Society.)

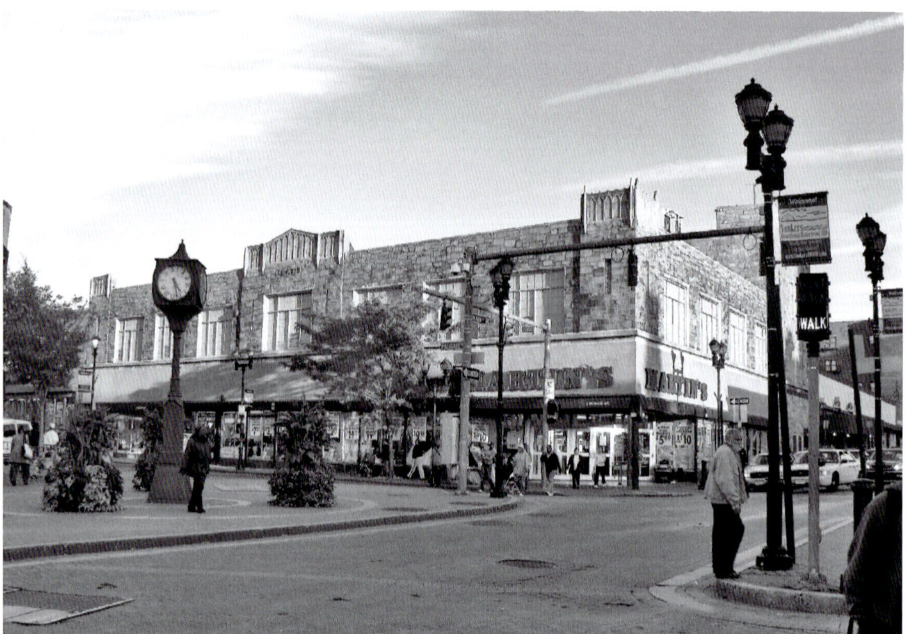

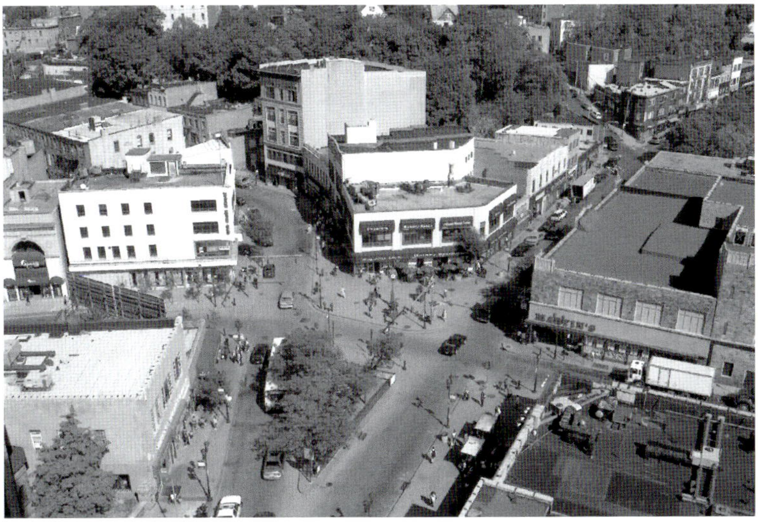

Getty Square is named after Robert Parkhill Getty, a successful New York businessman and Yonkers resident, whose hotel, the Getty House, dominated the square for many years. The square was the center of activity in Yonkers from its early days. In the 19th century, it developed into a commercial district, supported by Yonkers's growing residential suburbs. In 1888, Yonkers was a city of 19,000 people, most of whom lived within walking distance of the square. (Courtesy of Donald Kreutzberg.)

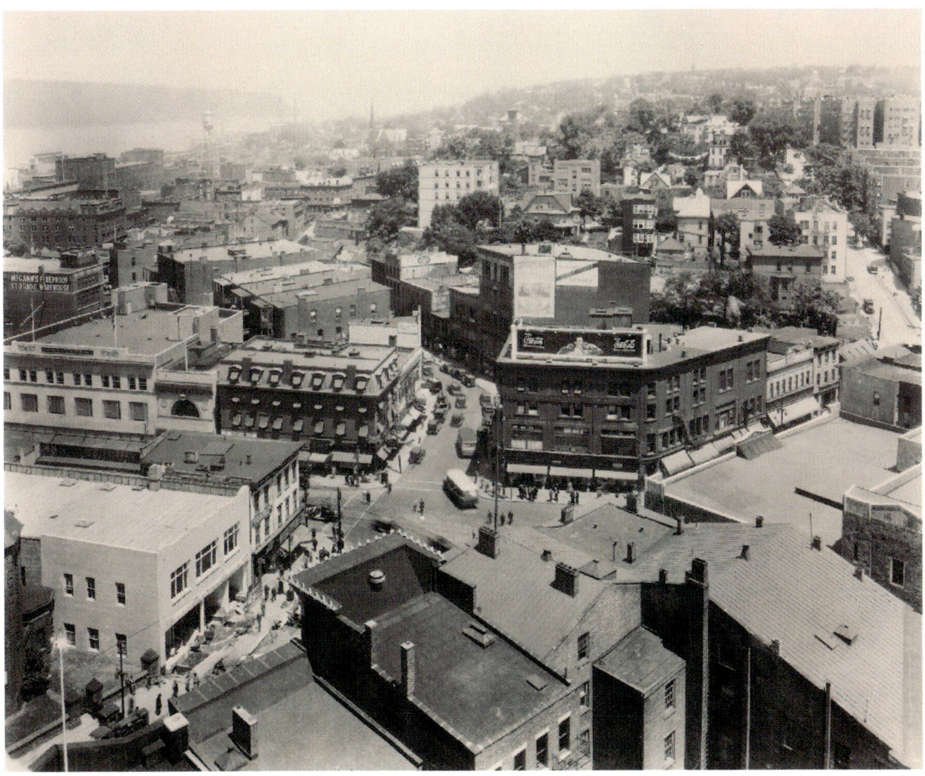

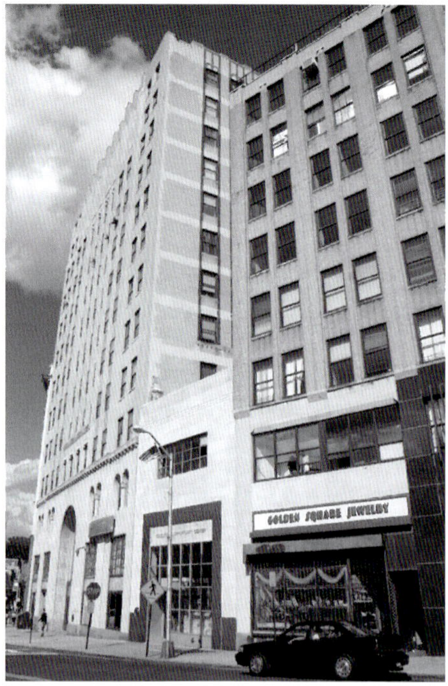

Designed by local architect William P. Katz for the First National Bank and Trust Company, 20 South Broadway was the city's tallest office building upon opening in 1931. Symbols of commerce and industry decorate the entrance arch and lobby. Train service to 155th Street, begun in 1888, continued until 1943, as trains still came to the back of the new building. The manhole cover in front is a reminder of this train line that serviced downtown Yonkers. (Courtesy of Yonkers Historical Society.)

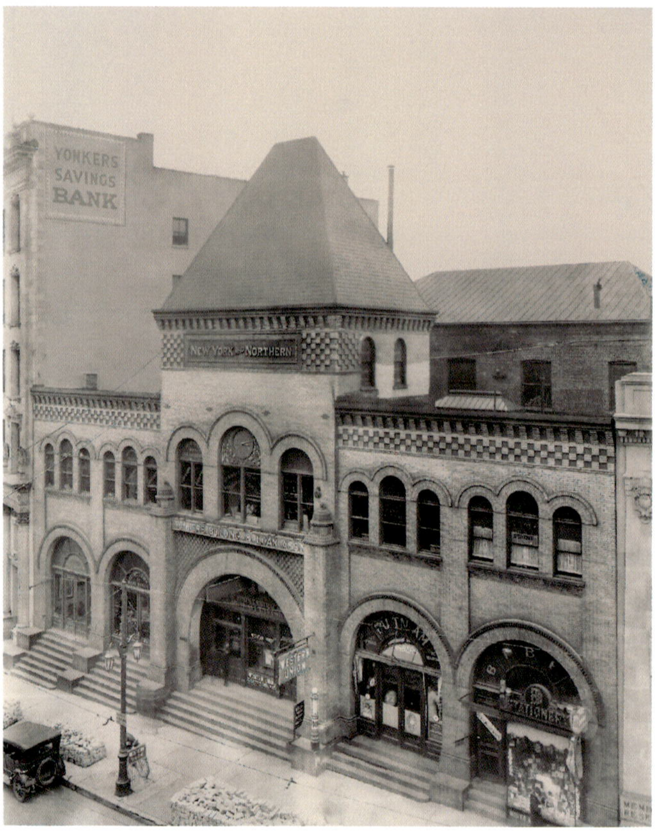

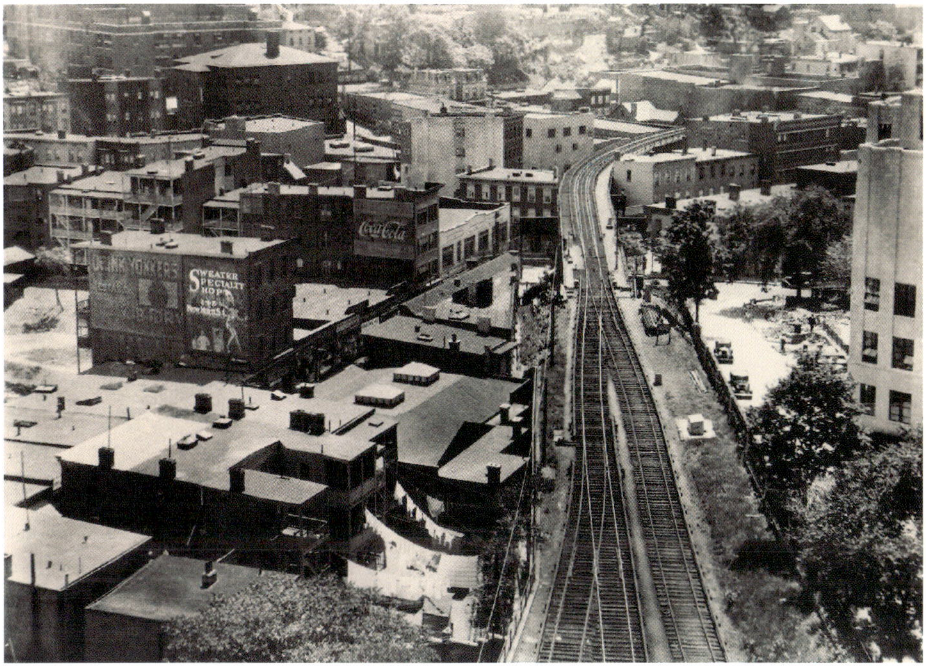

Tracks of the Putnam division of the New York and Northern Railroad extended from 155th Street to northern Westchester, but a 3.1-mile spur track broke off from the main line in the area of Van Cortlandt Park in the Bronx to service Yonkers. In addition to the two-story Getty Square terminal at 20 South Broadway (replaced by a bank building in 1931), there were three Yonkers stations on the spur, Caryl Avenue, Lowerre, and Park Hill. Train service, which began in March 1888, ended on June 30, 1943. (Courtesy of Yonkers Historical Society.)

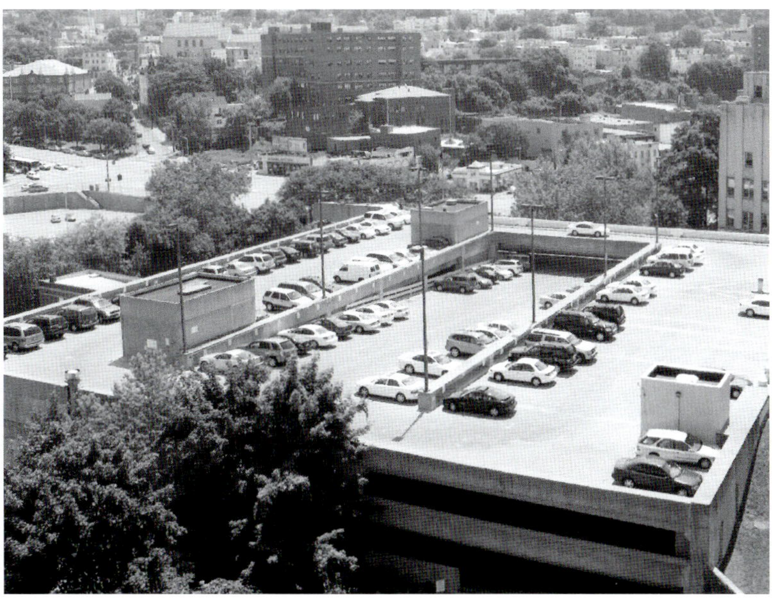

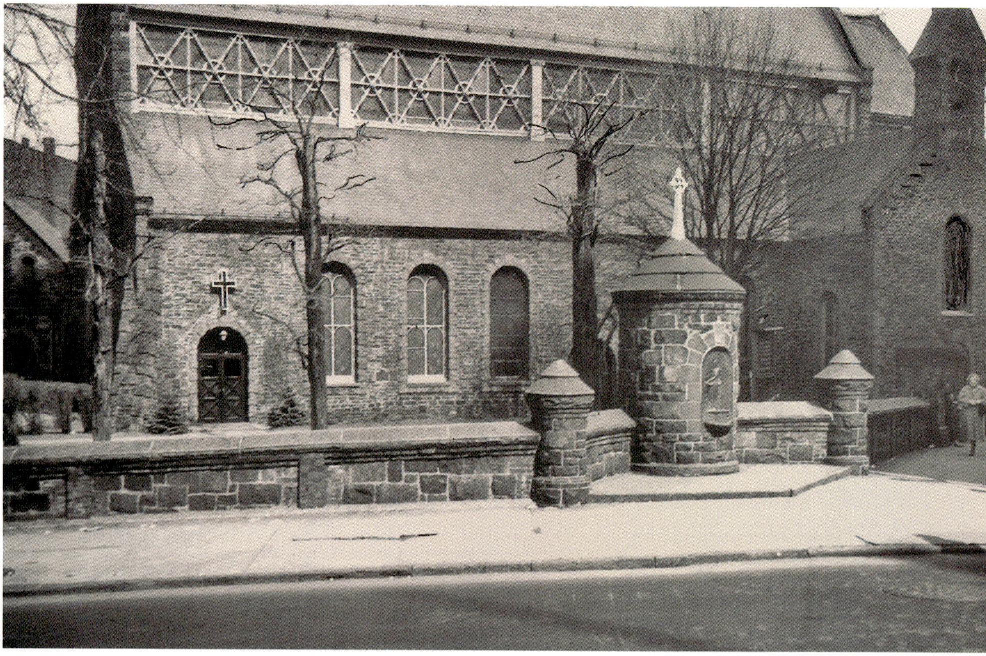

Founded in 1693 by an act of the British Crown, St. John's Episcopal Church is the oldest house of worship in Yonkers. The first church was constructed in 1752. During the Revolutionary War, St. John's served as a hospital. British and American soldiers are buried beneath its floors. In 1872, a new church was built in Colonial Revival style that retained the old south wall from the 1752 building. In 1891, a stone and brick wall with a corner ice fountain was erected around the two-acre site. (Courtesy of Yonkers Historical Society.)

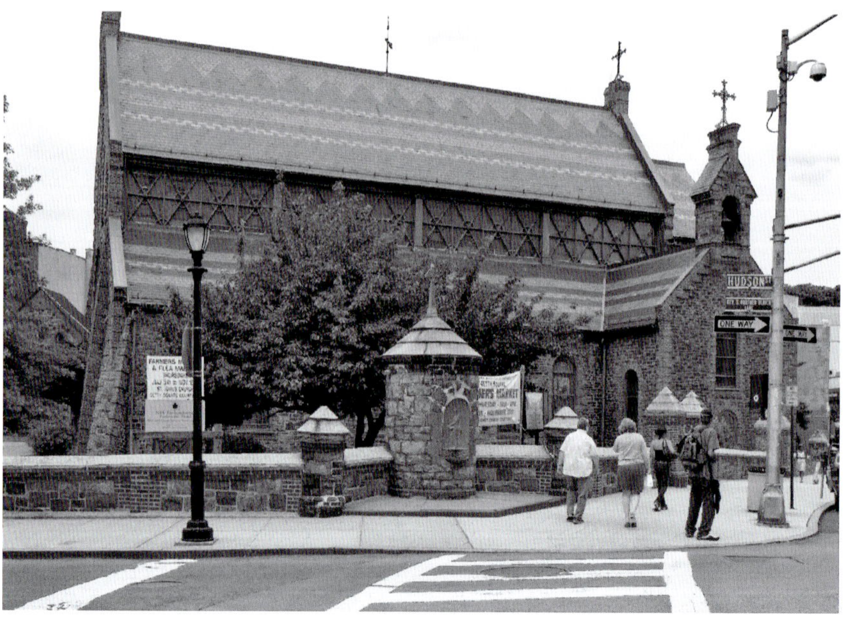

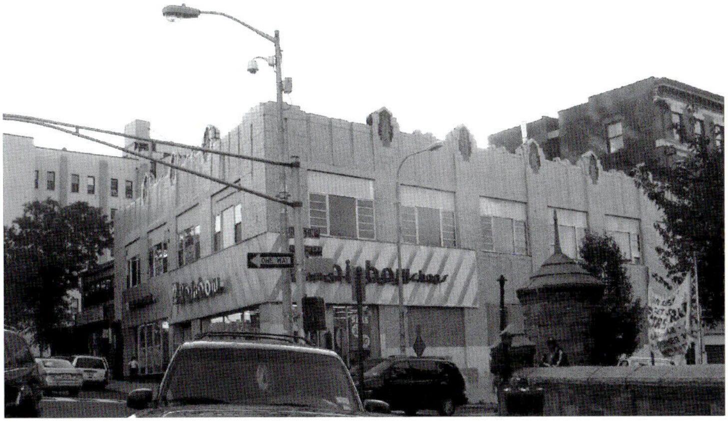

Standing on the southwest corner of Hudson Street and South Broadway, the Hollywood Inn was built as a clubhouse for workingmen to provide an alternative to the saloon. It opened on September 16, 1897. It was a gift to the city from William F. Cochran, an executive of the Alexander Smith Carpet Company in Yonkers. Cochran donated most of the $120,000 needed to build it, in addition to $10,000 for the free circulating library. Classrooms, a gymnasium, a bowling alley, and a billiard room were among the five-story building's amenities. It was demolished in 1933. (Courtesy of Yonkers Historical Society.)

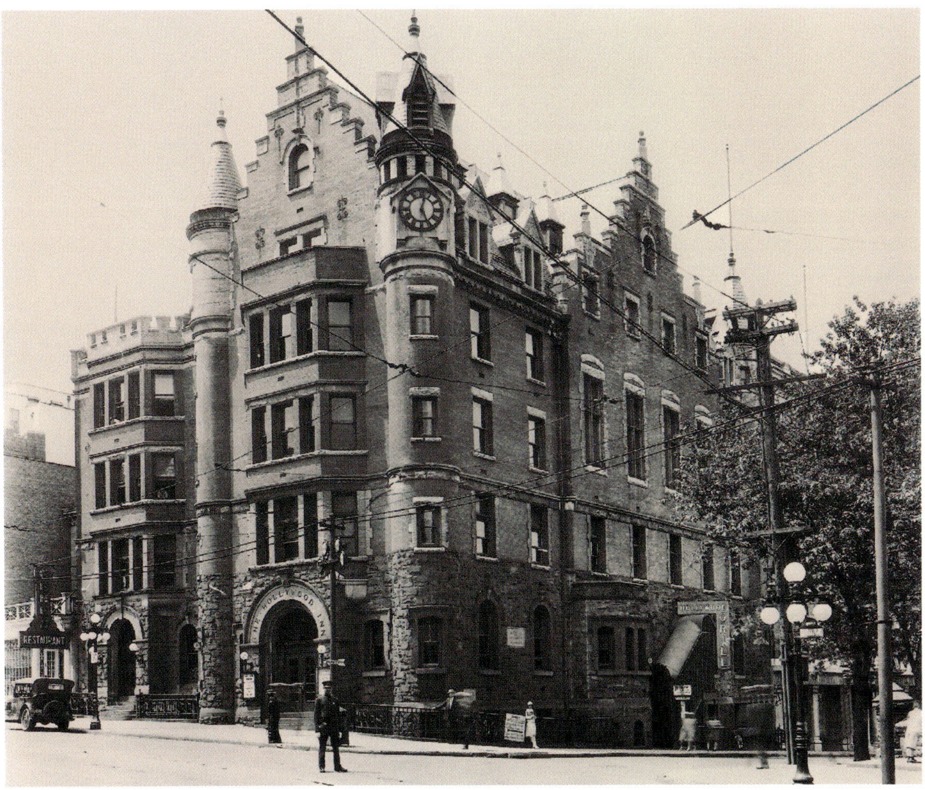

Founded in January 1887 by Adolph Klein, Ohab Zedek was the first permanent synagogue in Westchester. Initially called Congregation Sons of Israel, it incorporated as Congregation Ohab Zedek in 1902. In 1903, it constructed a building on Prospect Street that was a showcase for traditional Judaism and Hungarian formality. For a century, Ohab Zedek remained a touchstone of Yonkers orthodoxy. Demographic changes led to a merger that formed Young Israel-Ohab Zedek in Riverdale. The Prospect Street building was demolished, but a plaque marks the site. (Courtesy of Yonkers Historical Society.)

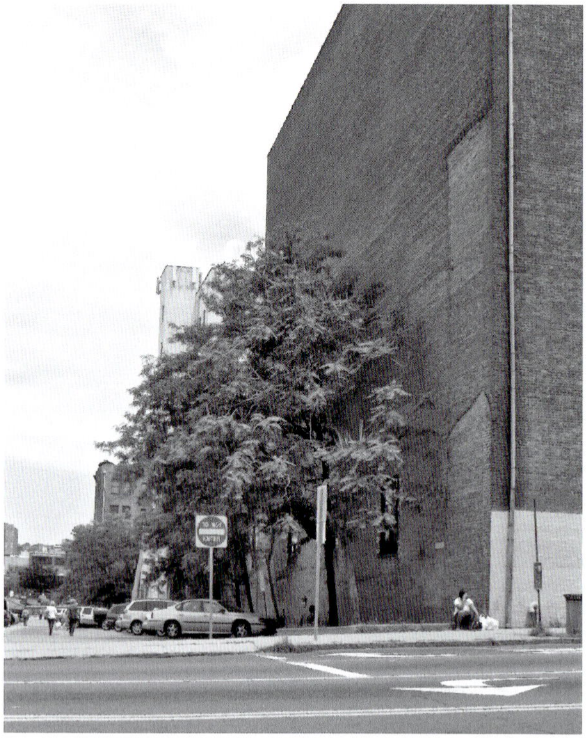

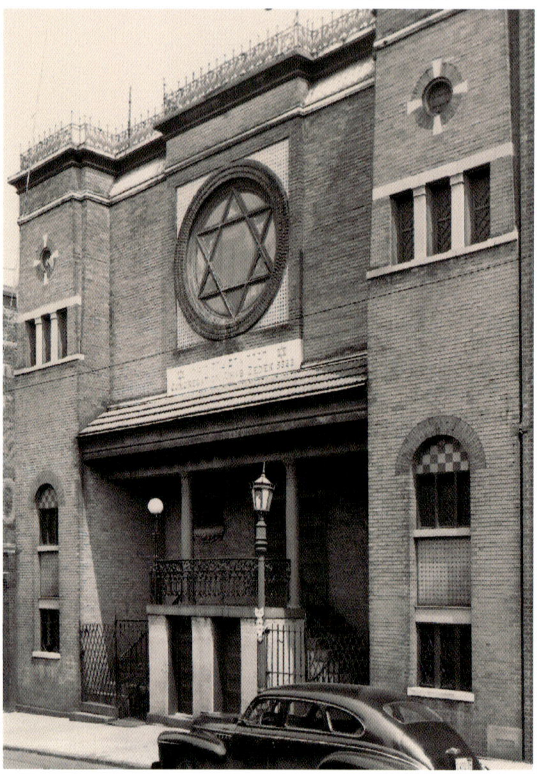

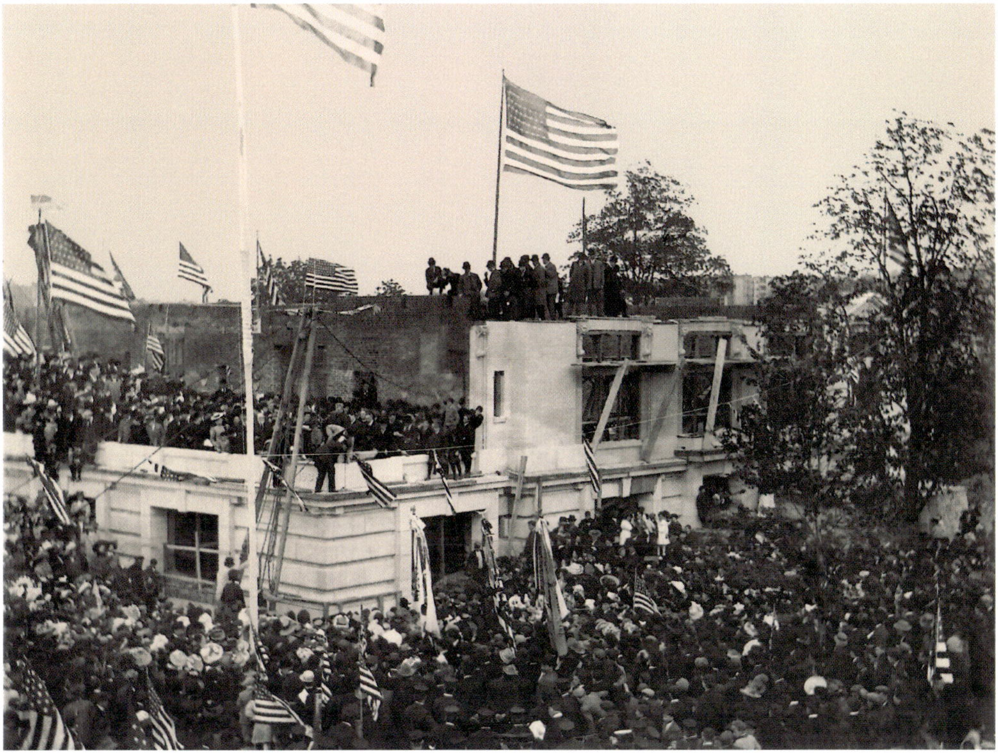

Overlooking Washington Park and dominating South Broadway, the Yonkers City Hall was designed by local architects Edwin A. and H. Lansing Quick. Ground was broken in 1907. The laying of the cornerstone is seen here. Yonkers builder George T. Kelly constructed the building and finished it in 1910. The National Register of Historic Places Building Inventory form for the building references it as "a free interpretation of Neo-Baroque forms." The domed clock tower, rising 100 feet above the ground, is visible for miles. (Courtesy of the Hudson River Museum.)

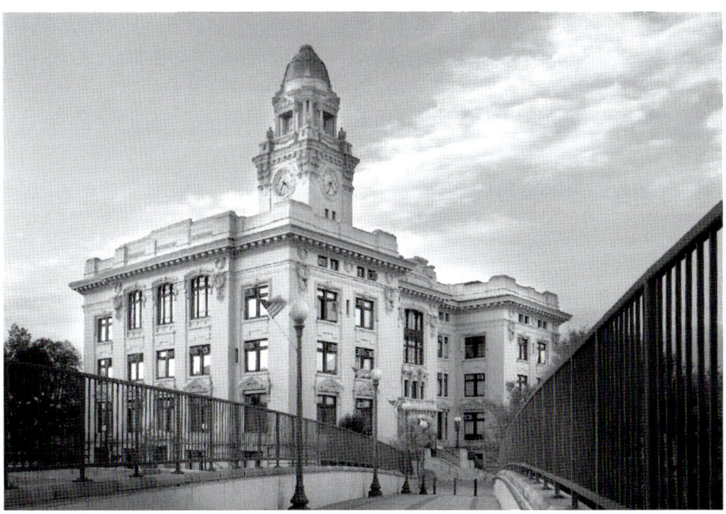

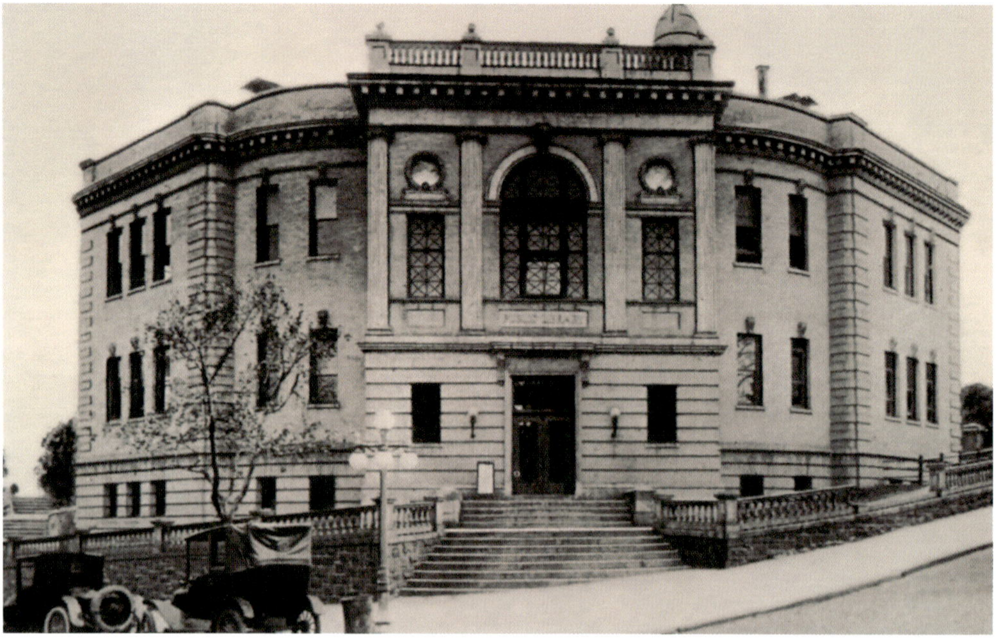

Gracing the corner of Nepperhan Avenue and South Broadway, the main branch of the Yonkers Public Library was built in 1903 with $50,000 donated by philanthropist Andrew Carnegie. Designed by Yonkers architects and built by a local builder, the building was elliptical in shape, the best style to fit the corner of a hill. The beautiful staircases were made of white Tuckahoe marble. Despite public outcry, the Carnegie library was demolished in May 1982 to make way for improvements to Nepperhan Avenue. (Courtesy of Yonkers Historical Society.)

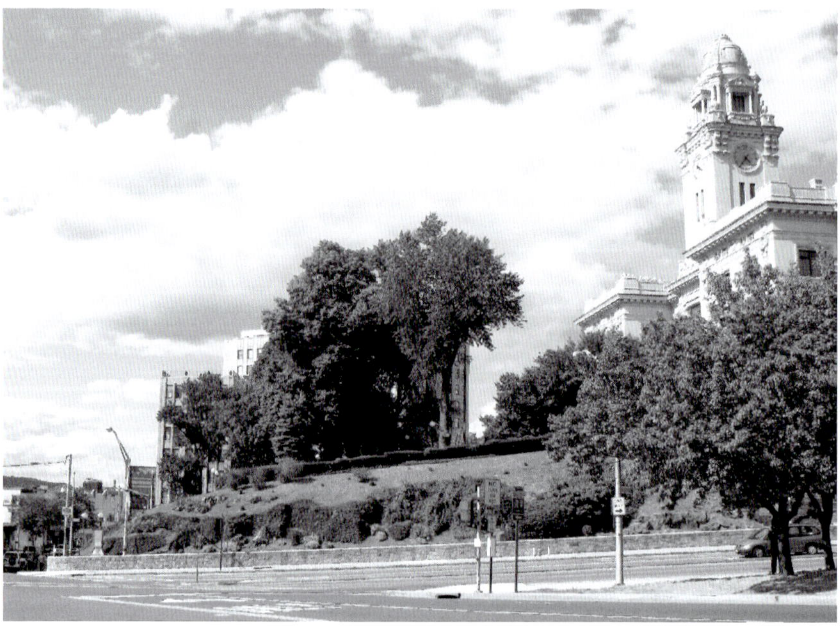

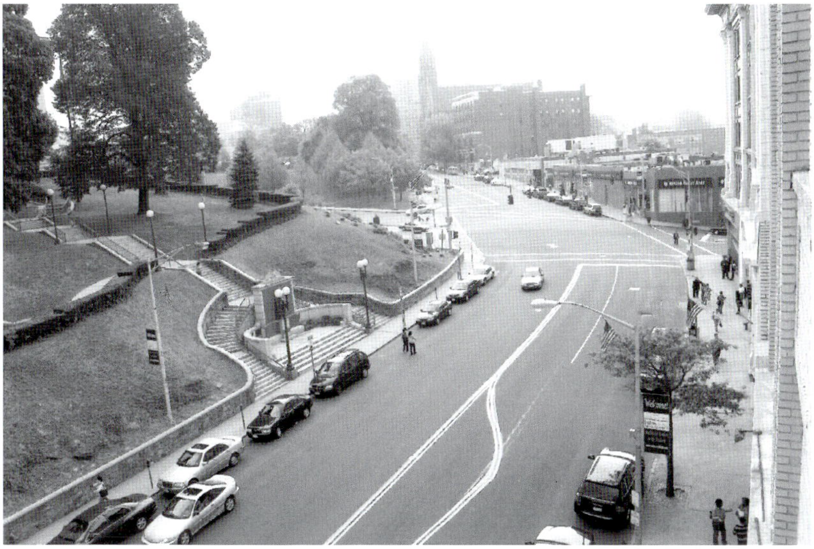

Running from the Bronx border at the south to the Hastings line at the north, the old Albany Post Road—now known as Broadway, or, more precisely, South Broadway below Getty Square and North Broadway above the square—bisects the whole of west Yonkers. One of the oldest trails in America, it was also a stagecoach route. Seen here is the stretch of South Broadway immediately to the west of Yonkers City Hall. (Courtesy of Yonkers Historical Society.)

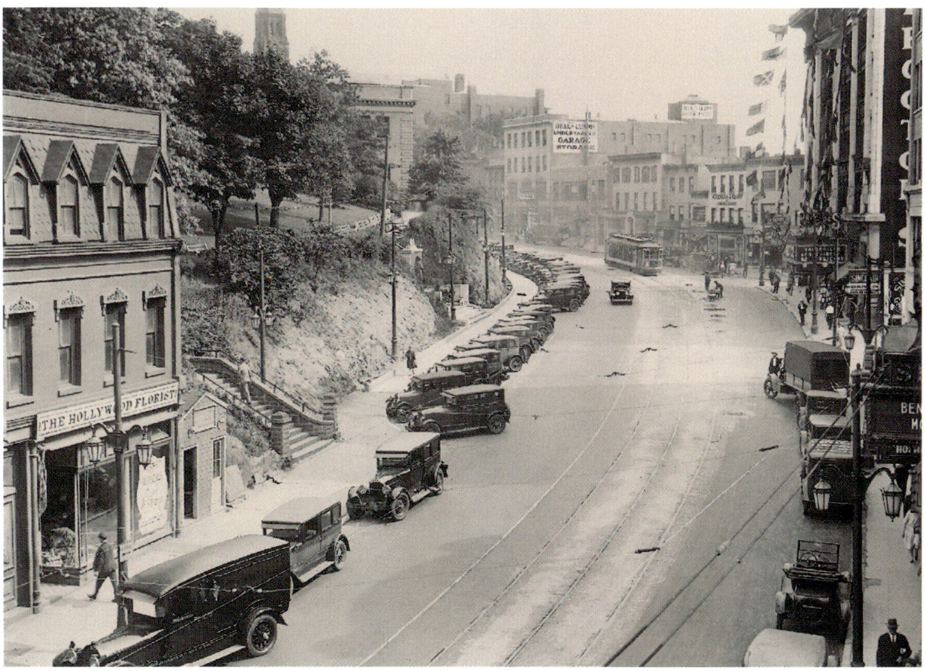

The Church of the Immaculate Conception, familiarly known as St. Mary's, is the oldest Catholic Church in Yonkers, having been established in 1848. The first mass was celebrated in the practically completed redbrick building on Christmas Day of that year. On May 4, 1890, a ceremony was held for the laying of the cornerstone of the present church, located at the corner of South Broadway and St. Mary's Street. It took over two years to complete the new church, which was dedicated by Archbishop Michael Corrigan in 1892. A new stone altar made from local quarry to honor the memory of the first parishioners was installed in 1998 on the parish's 150th anniversary. (Courtesy of Immaculate Conception Church of Saint Mary's.)

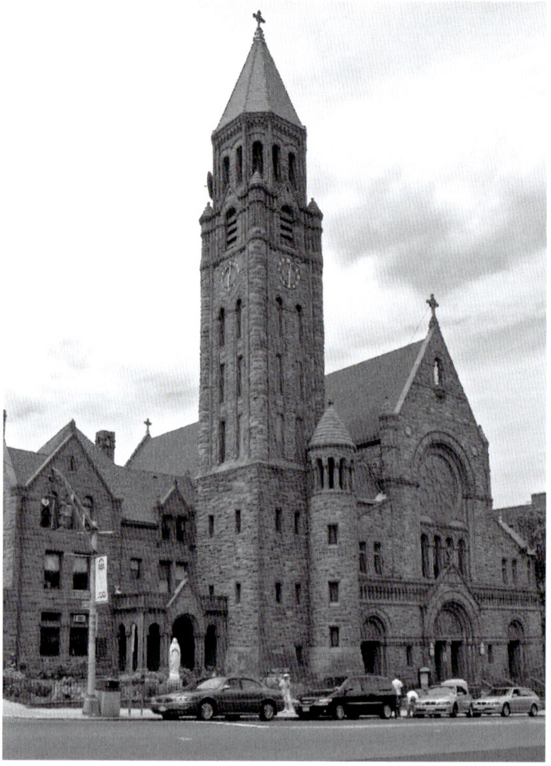

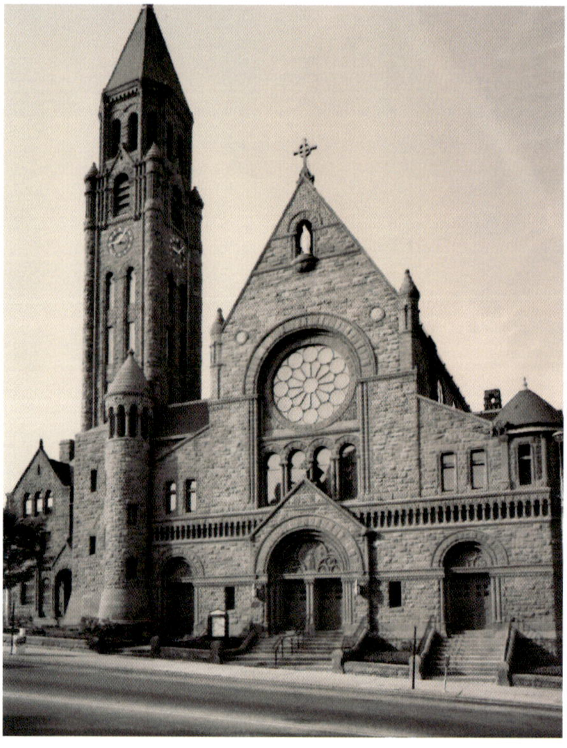

CHAPTER

SOUTHWEST YONKERS

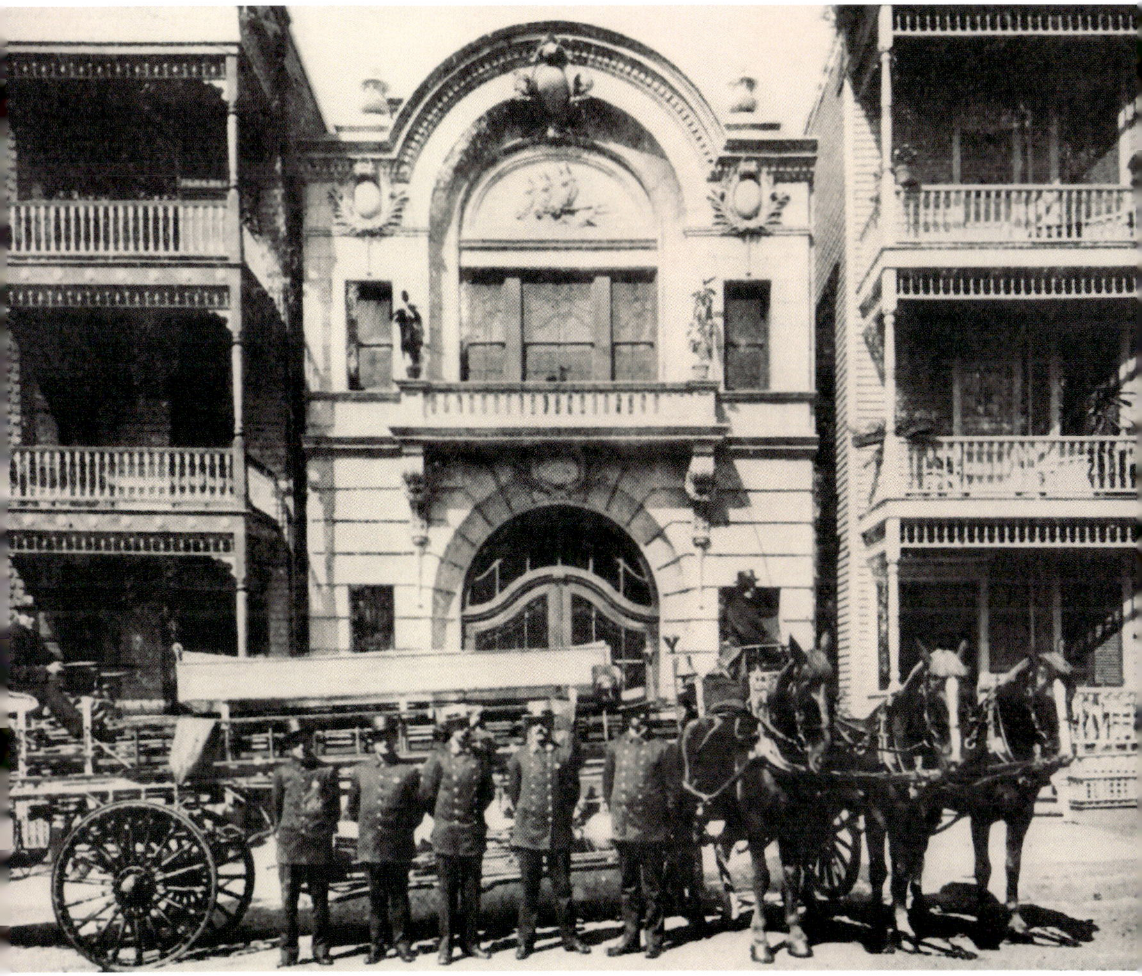

In 1896, the city's paid fire department was officially organized. From that day forward, the Yonkers Fire Department grew to what it is today. In 1900, money was authorized to erect a new firehouse in the Fifth Ward. The firehouse at Oak and Ash Streets was built in 1901. Benjamin Franklin, a champion of volunteer firefighting, perhaps said it best when he called fire "a good servant but a terrible master." (Courtesy of Donald Kreutzberg.)

The stately Nodine Hill water tower was built in 1891 and remained in use for 46 years, until 1937 when the 175-foot brick tower collapsed. The metal tank in the tower ruptured, and bricks and steel fell earthward, loosing 100,000 gallons of water. The water swept wreckage in a solid wall downhill to Getty Square. Many were injured but, miraculously, no one was killed. Several homes on the streets were caved in and cars crushed. (Courtesy of Yonkers Historical Society.)

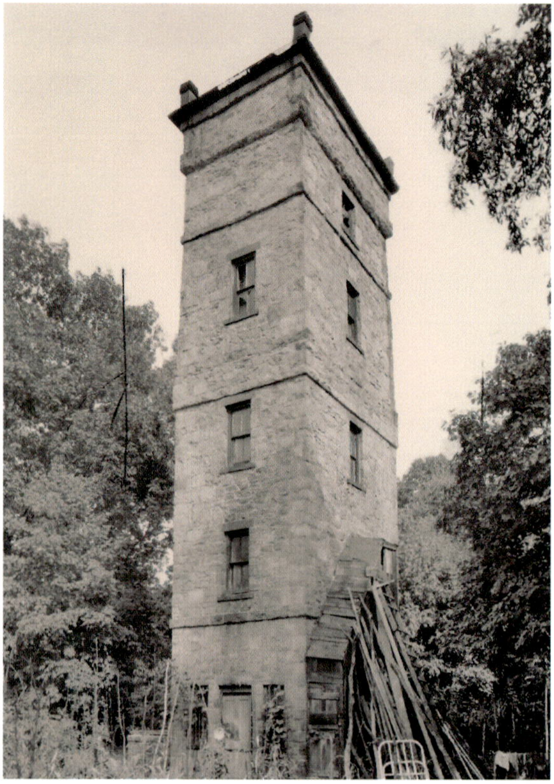

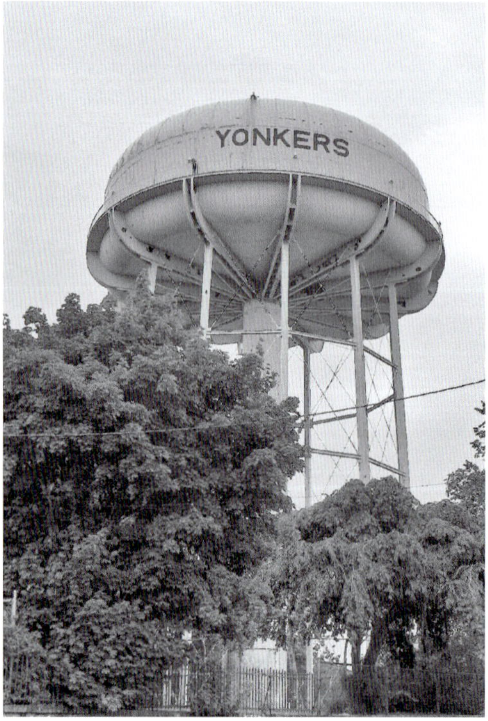

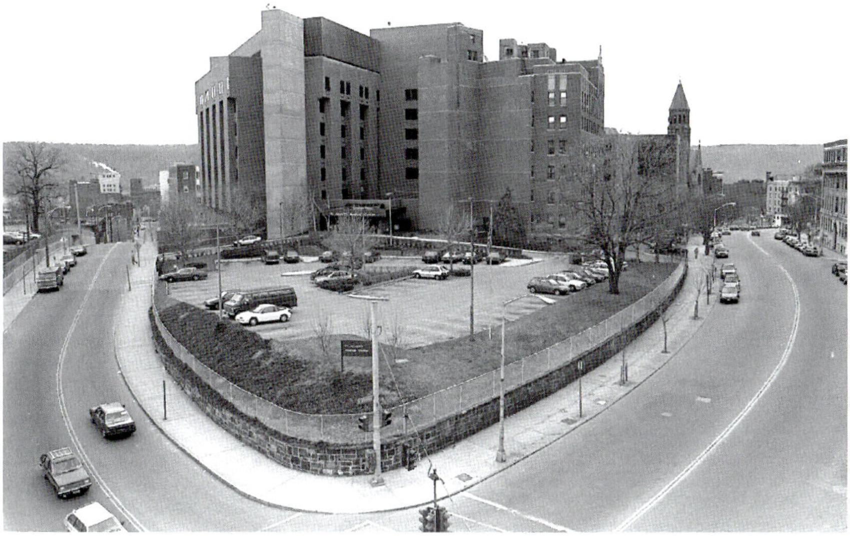

Founded in 1888 by the Sisters of Charity of St. Vincent DePaul of New York and occupying the site of the former St. Aloysius Academy on the corner of Vark Street and South Broadway, St. Joseph's Hospital (now known as St. Joseph's Medical Center) has been meeting the health care needs of the Yonkers area ever since. In 1979, a new hospital building was constructed on the site and the original hospital building demolished shortly thereafter. A nursing home was added in 1976. (Courtesy of Flynn Memorial Trust.)

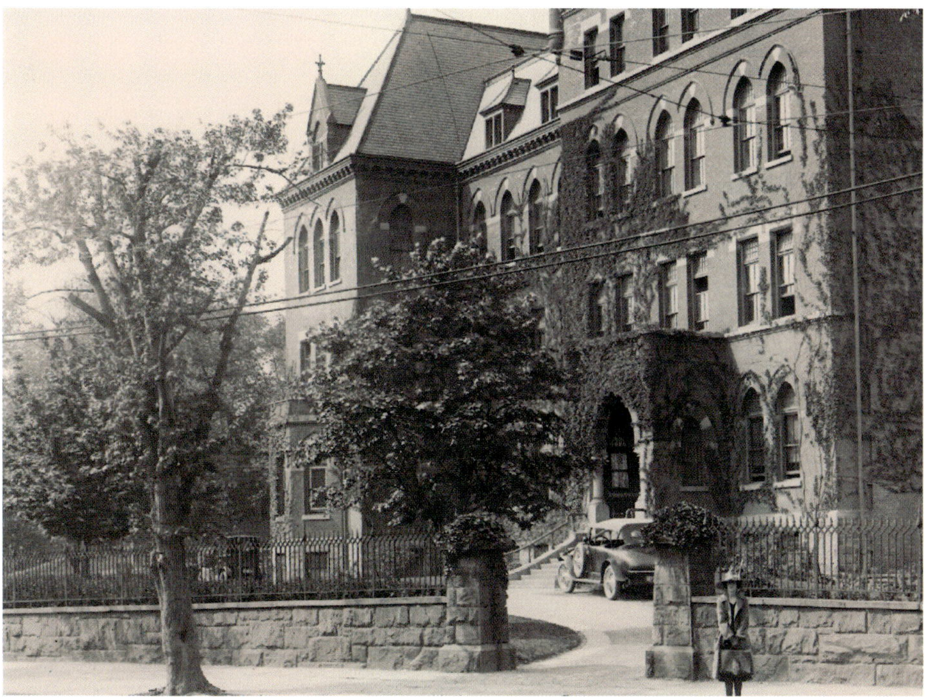

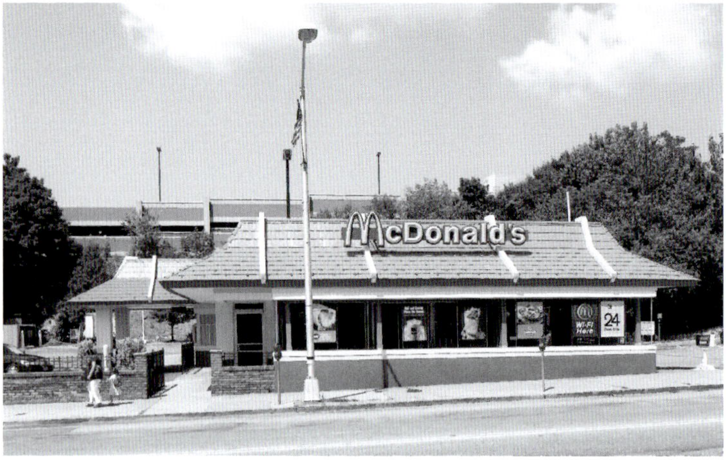

Built in the late 1920s by the Andrus family interests in arrangement with Loews Theaters, the Loew's on South Broadway and Vark Street was one of the largest and finest movie palaces in the entire region. It was the latest in theater construction. The predominant style of the interior was art deco, which enjoyed something of a nostalgic revival in the 1970s. In the 1950s, it became Brandt's Theatre but was demolished in 1975. (Courtesy of Yonkers Planning Bureau.)

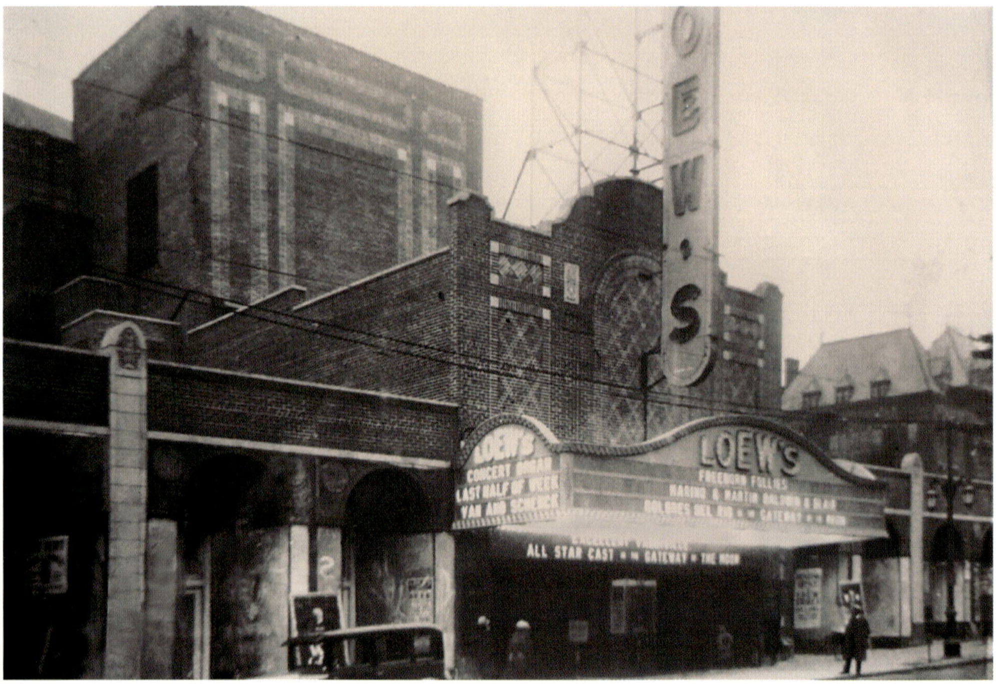

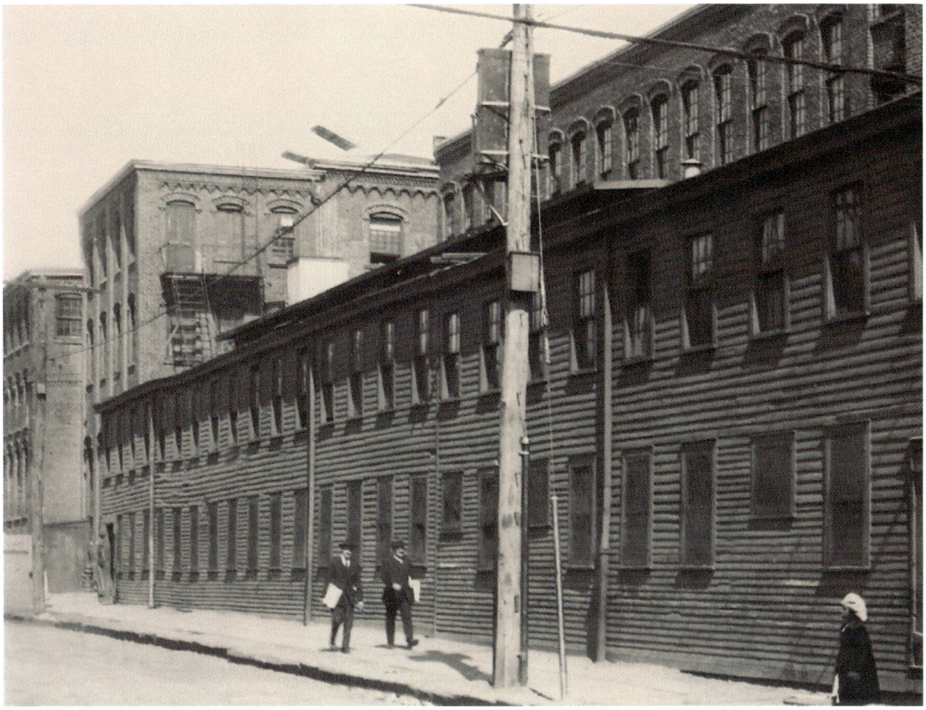

The hat industry in Yonkers dates from 1828. Various members of the Waring family were engaged in the business at different locations in the city. Shown here is the Waring Hat factory, which extended from South Broadway and Vark Street to Riverdale Avenue. It manufactured about 10,800 fur hats a day in the mid-1890s. The company also operated in two other locations closer to Getty Square. Constructed during the Civil War, the Vark Street building was originally owned by Starr Arms, a manufacturer of weapons for the Union army. John T. Waring purchased the building in the late 1870s. (Courtesy of Yonkers Historical Society.)

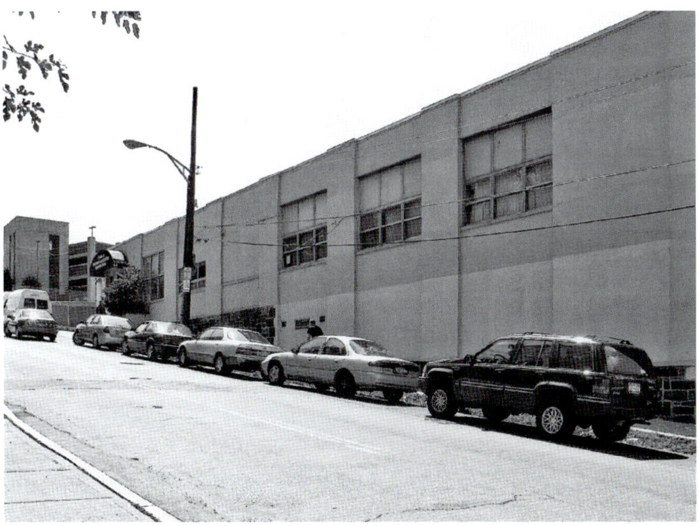

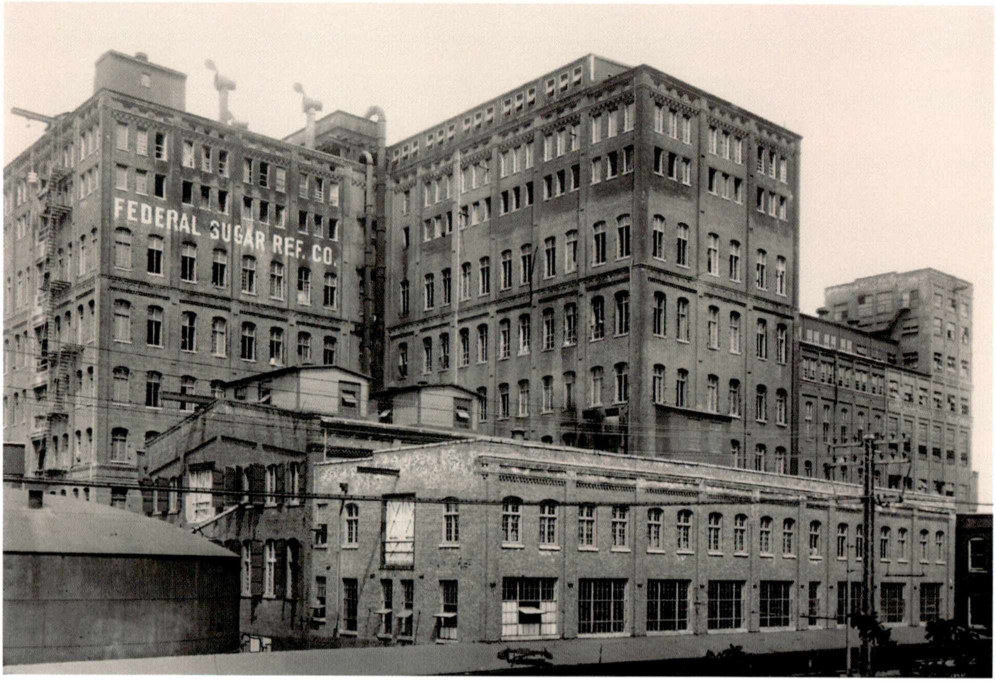

Fondly known to generations of residents as "the Sugar House," today's American Sugar Refining, located on the banks of the Hudson River south of downtown Yonkers, is the result of the consolidation of numerous sugar refineries, sugar syrup stations, and packing facilities. The sugar industry had its beginning in Yonkers in 1862. In 1863, a sugar factory was established, and in 1893, it reorganized as the National Sugar Refinery. It closed in 1931. In 1937 or 1938, Refined Sugars acquired the Yonkers property. Today this plant is the last surviving sugar refinery in the northeastern United States. (Courtesy of Yonkers Historical Society.)

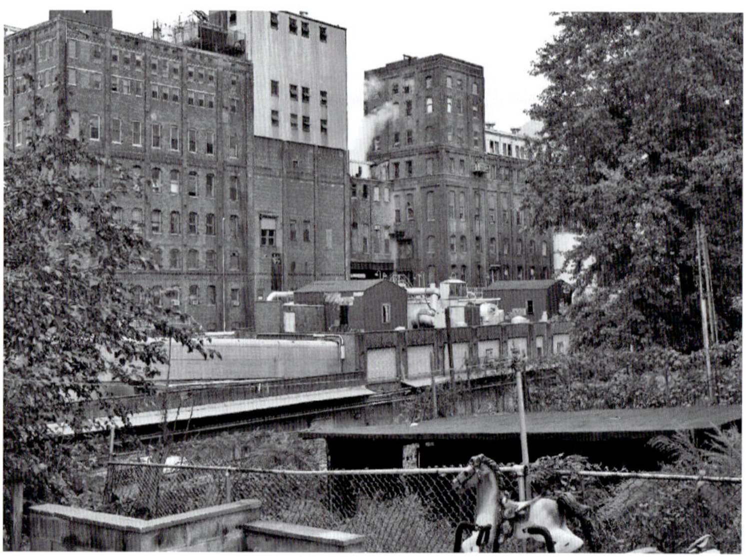

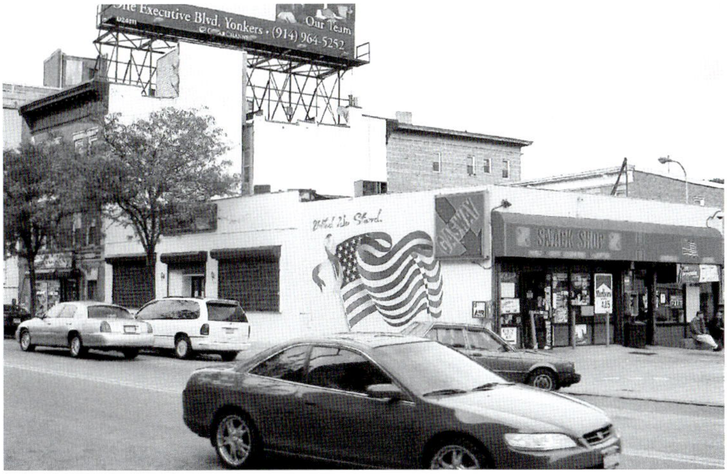

Francois Francfort opened the Francfort Inn on South Broadway and New Main Street in 1890. At the dawn of the 20th century and in the two decades that followed, the inn was a rendezvous for gourmets and distinguished visitors who were entertained there. The one-room restaurant was a landmark stop on the old coach route. In 1930, it was enlarged to double its space and became the French Chef, which became a landmark in its own right for the next four decades until its closing in 1970. (Courtesy of Mimi Welsh.)

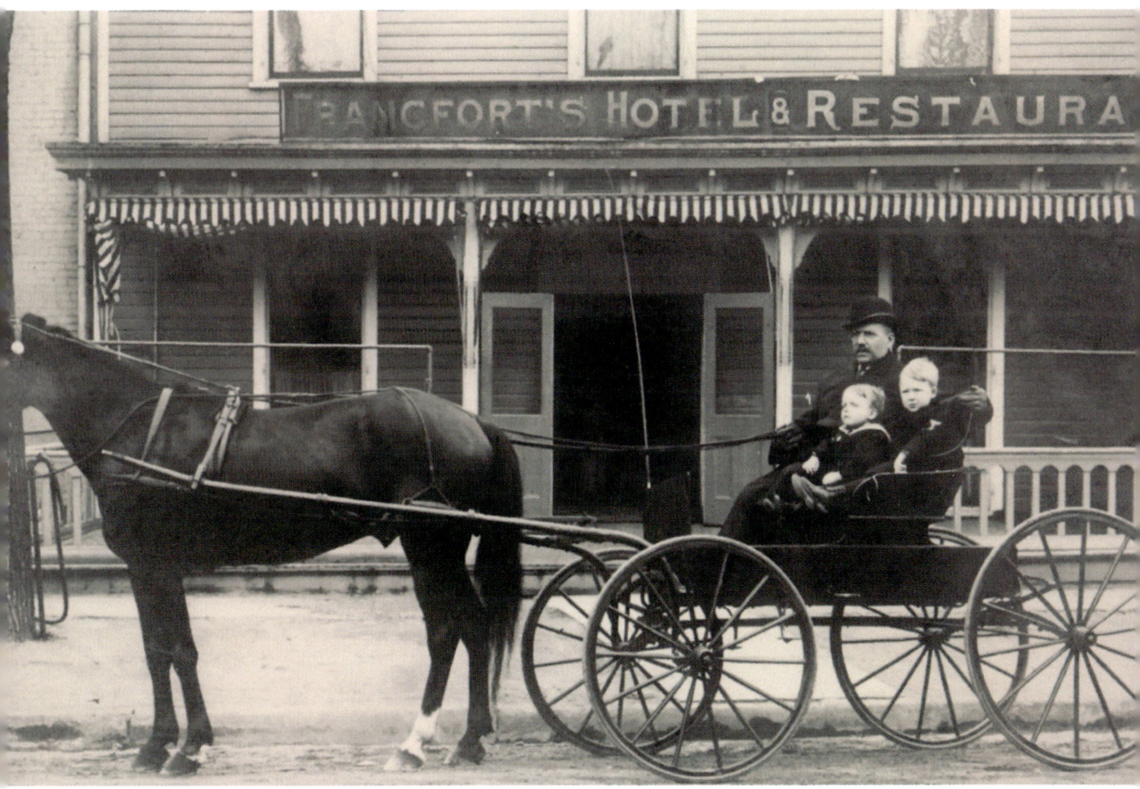

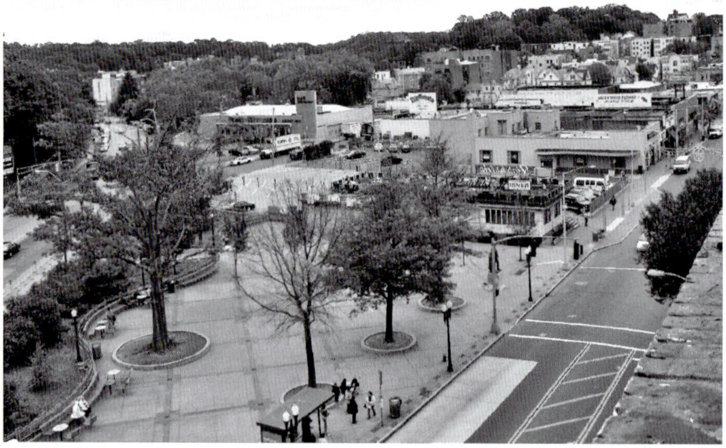

Originally acquired by the city for the purpose of memorializing Yonkers veterans of the Great War, Lincoln Park stands at the fork of South Broadway and McLean Avenue. Located in the park is a plaque in memory of the heroes of the war. The park is dominated by the bronze statue of Abraham Lincoln, the work of local sculptor Isidore Konti. (Courtesy of Yonkers Historical Society.)

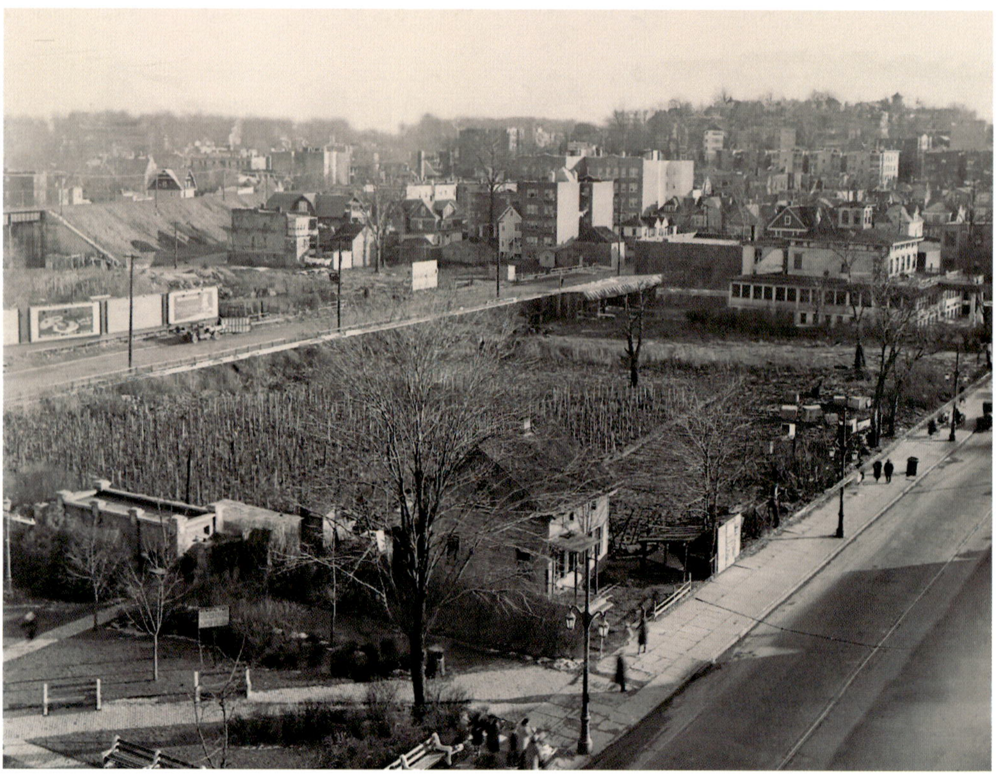

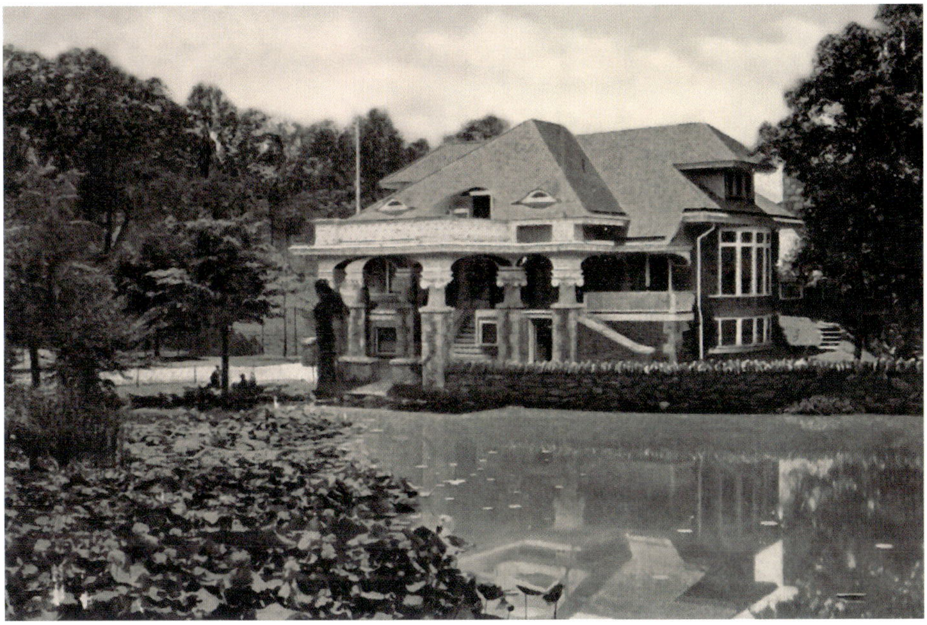

Park Hill, a stately 19th-century neighborhood, is on a 300-foot-high plateau overlooking the Hudson River. Developed in 1888, it was one of the first planned suburban communities in the area. The Racquet Club was first established as the Park Hill County Club in 1892. The original clubhouse was destroyed in a fire on March 1, 1962. The membership continued to meet on the grounds and, in the spirit of community that continues today, rebuilt this neighborhood institution. Decades later, the club continues to be a vital part of Park Hill and Yonkers, bringing families and friends together. (Courtesy of Rosalie Flynn.)

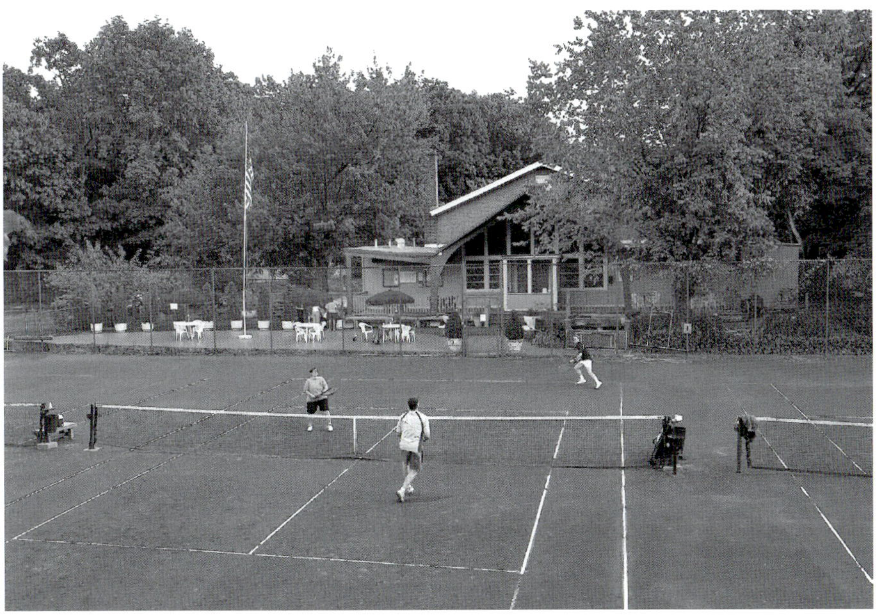

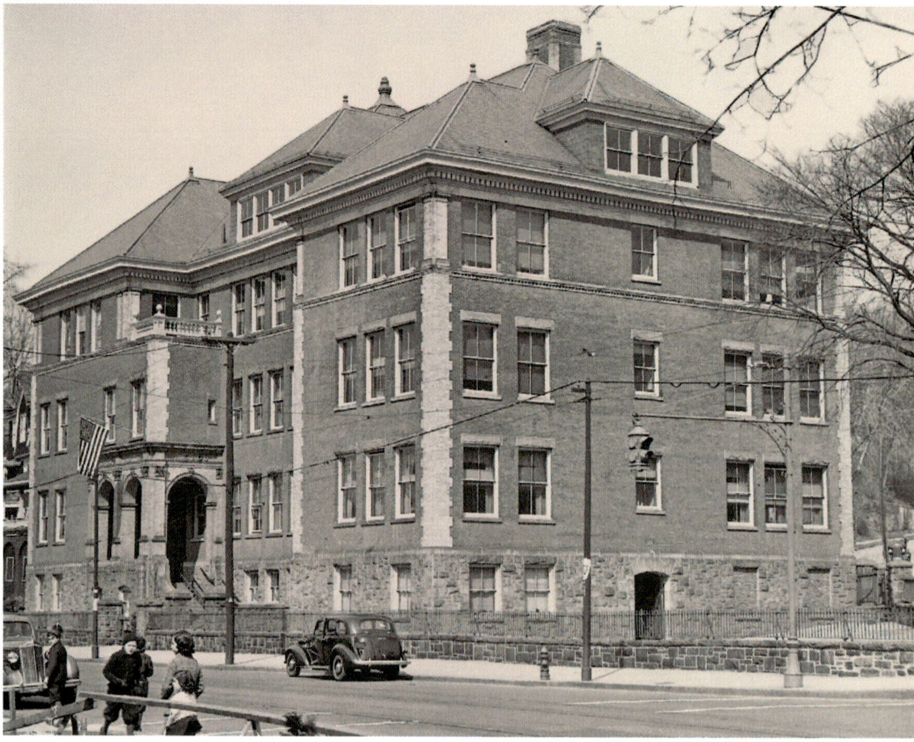

Public School 13, located at the corner of McLean Avenue and Park Hill Avenue, opened in 1900. It originally had five classrooms, an auditorium, and an office. Its rural location was considered at the time as out of the way, and there were neither trolleys nor buses to transport the students to and from school. The school building was recently renovated and converted into apartments. (Courtesy of Westchester County Historical Society.)

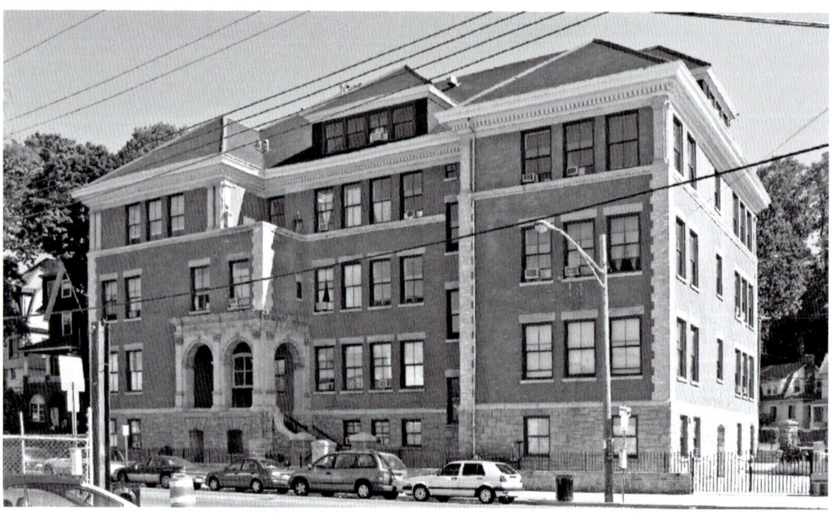

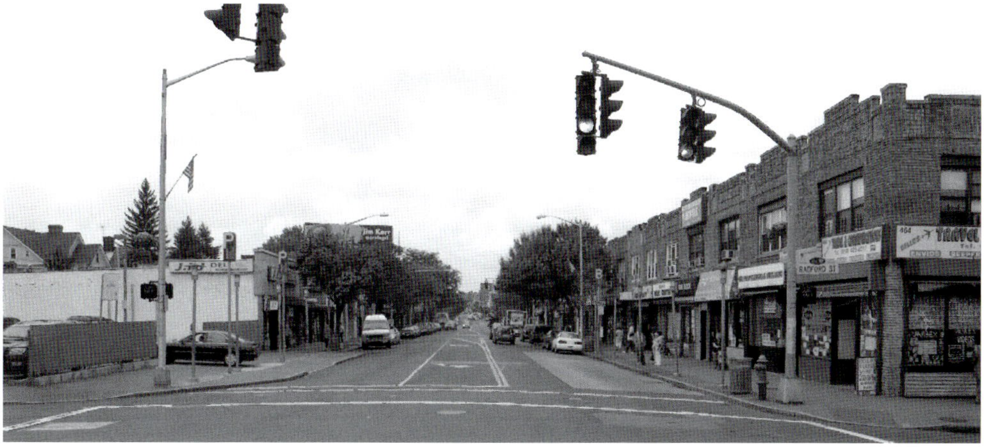

South Broadway is the oldest path, trail, road, highway, and street in Yonkers. It was first an animal path, a Native American trail, and a country road. In 1669, it was opened as a through route from Manhattan Island to Philipse Manor. In 1785, the stagecoach using this route took five hours to get from Yonkers to New York via Kingsbridge. (Courtesy of Yonkers Historical Society.)

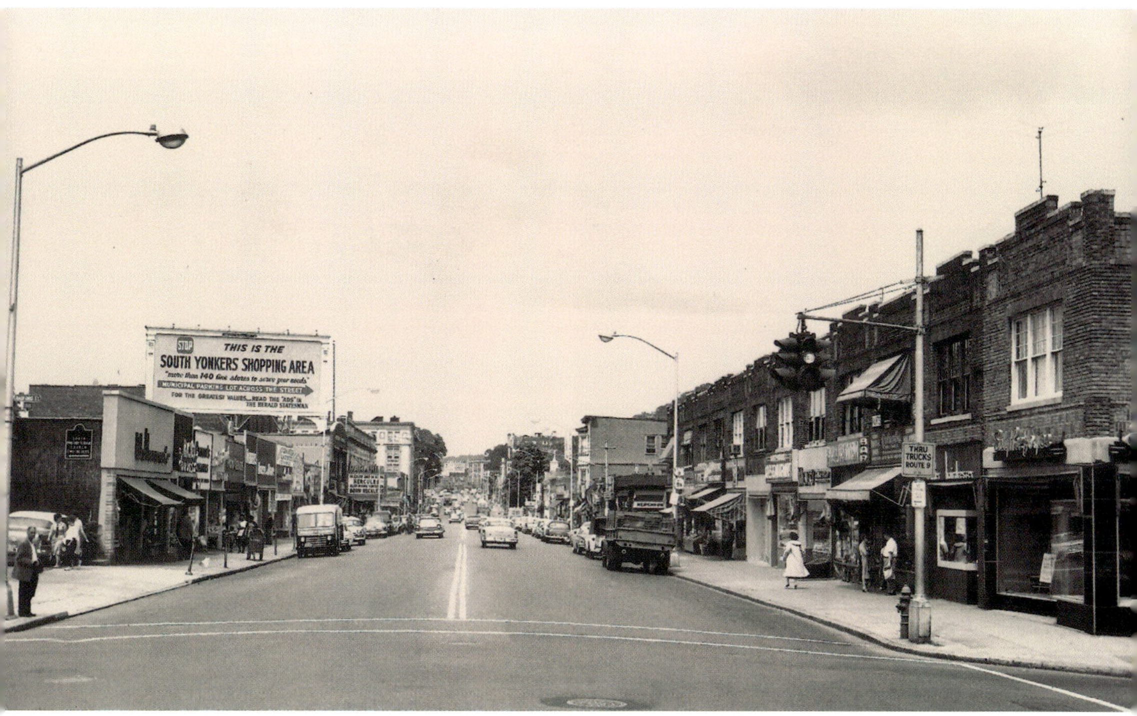

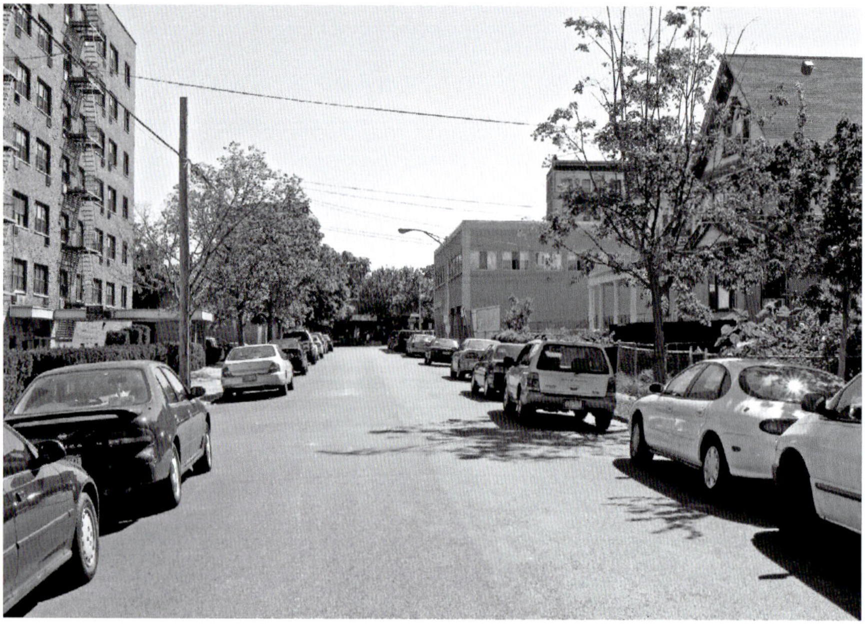

St. Andrews Place was once a single-family residential street. Former mayor Leslie Sutherland and wife resided as 66 St. Andrews Place. He was quoted as saying he lived "in the house on the hill by the side of the road." He was mayor from 1897 to 1901 and was then elected as county clerk of Westchester. St. Andrews Place has since evolved into a mix of apartment buildings and two-family homes. (Courtesy of Yonkers Historical Society.)

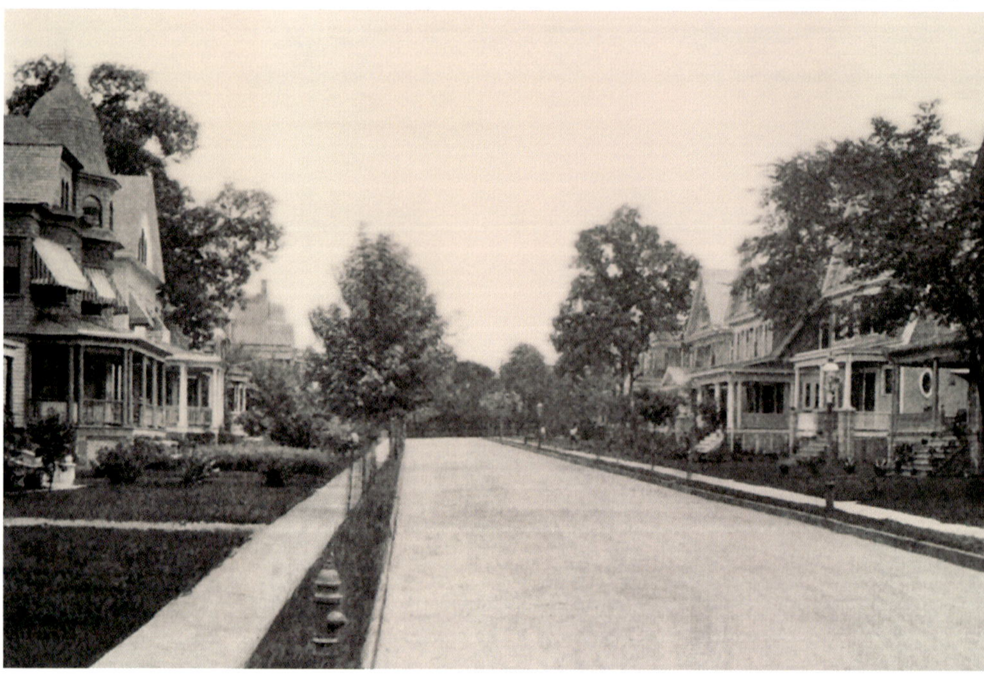

CHAPTER

NORTHWEST YONKERS

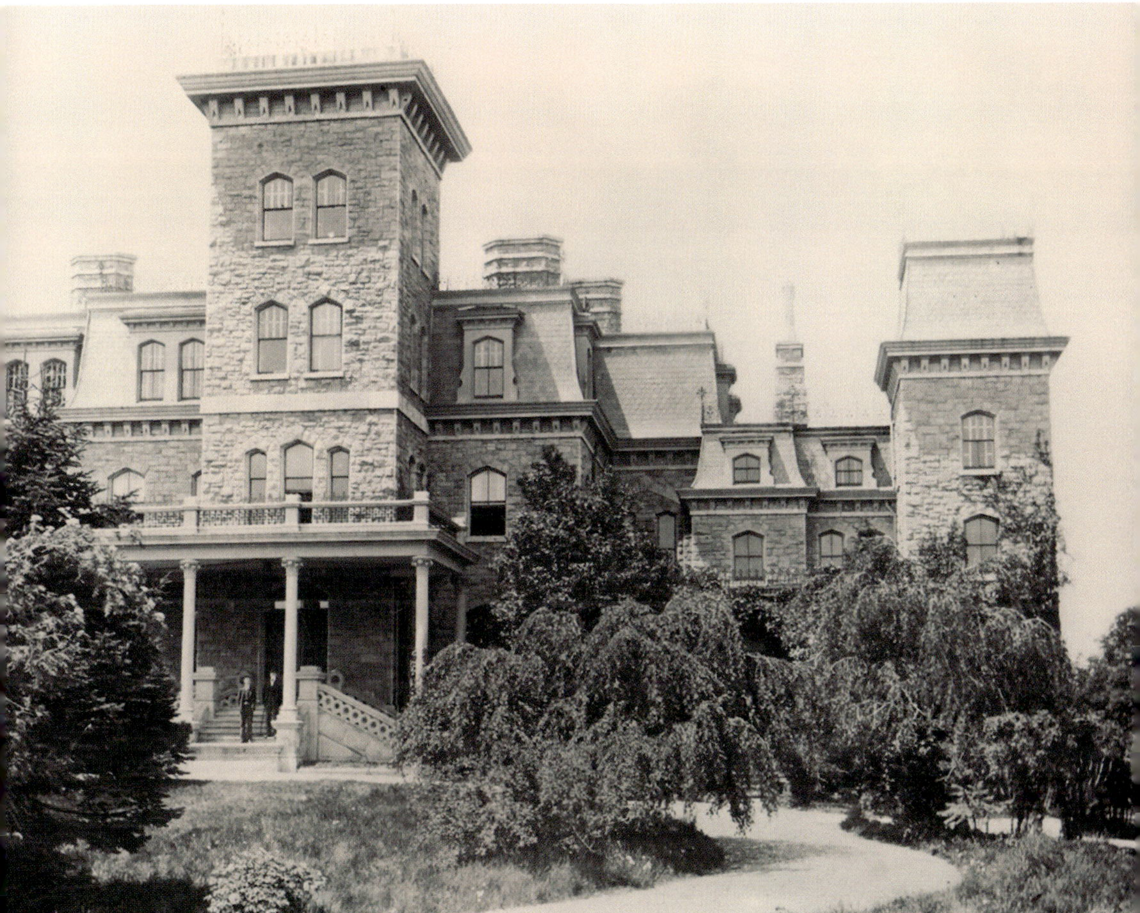

Greystone was built for hat manufacturer John T. Waring in 1868. After suffering heavy financial loses in 1876, he sold the mansion to Samuel J. Tilden, who won the popular vote as the Democratic candidate for president that same year. Tilden retired to Yonkers and moved into Greystone in 1879. Greystone was bought by Samuel Untermyer, a successful lawyer, in 1899. The house was demolished in the 1950s, and today Untermyer Park marks the site of the mansion with part of its formal gardens. (Courtesy of Yonkers Historical Society.)

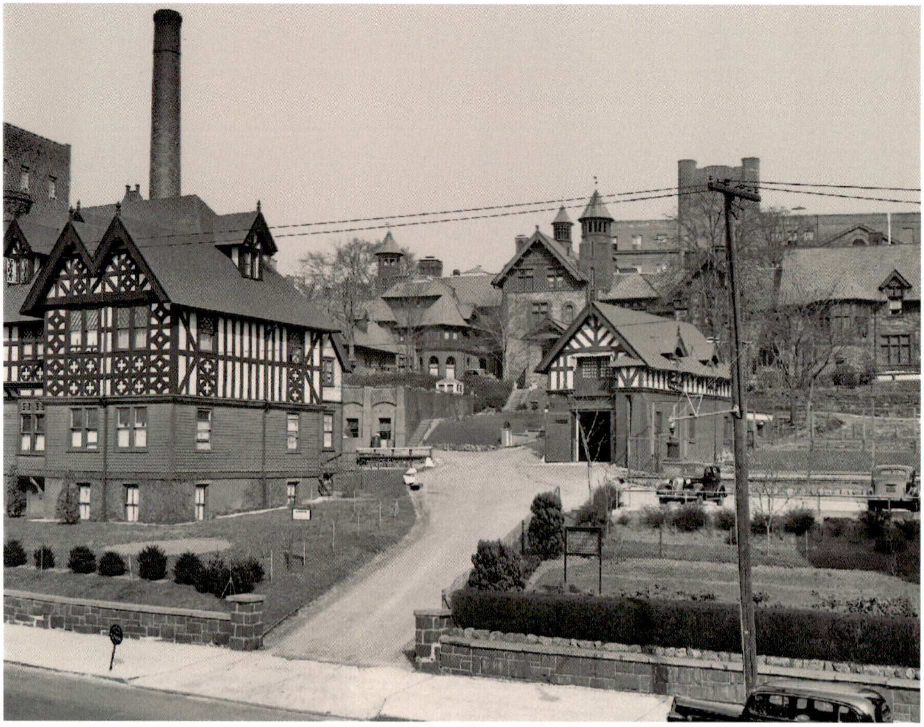

In 1869, a small, dedicated committee of women from St. John's Episcopal Church opened the St. John's Invalid Home. Officially incorporated as a charitable institute in early 1870, St. John's became the first hospital in Westchester County. In 1894, William and Eva Cochran donated buildings and further increased capacity to 100 beds. With help from the Andrus family and the Surdna Foundation, St. John's moved to its present 14-story, 273-bed hospital facility on North Broadway in 1963. (Courtesy of Hudson River Museum.)

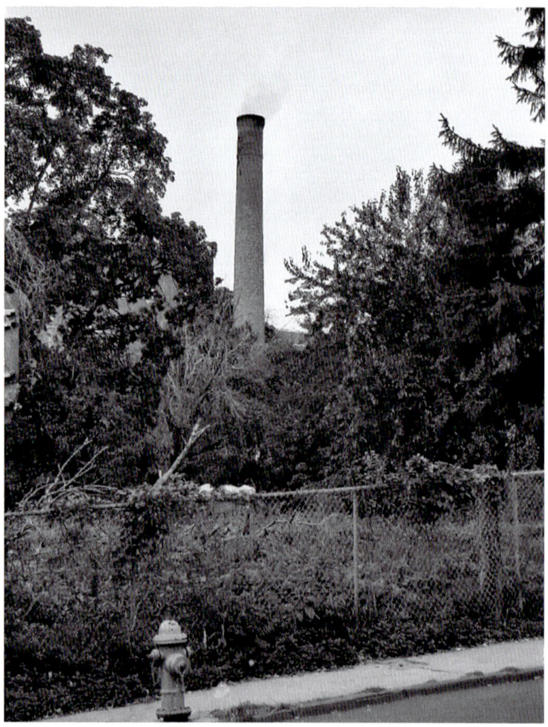

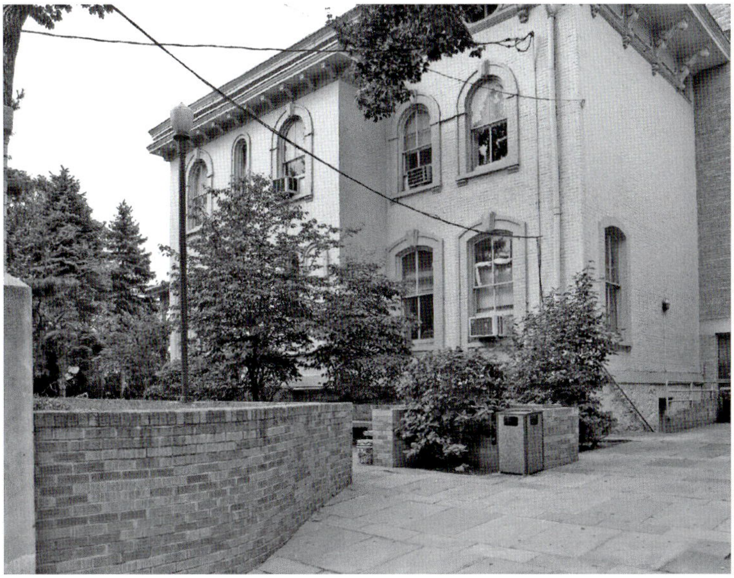

Oak Hill at 23 Park Avenue, was originally the home of Ethan Flagg, a prominent local citizen who was both a village trustee and president of the first bank to be incorporated in Yonkers. It was built sometime in the late 1850s. It later became the Convent of the Blessed Sacrament. The academy and convent closed in 1975. The building is presently owned by the Greystone Foundation. (Courtesy of Hudson River Museum.)

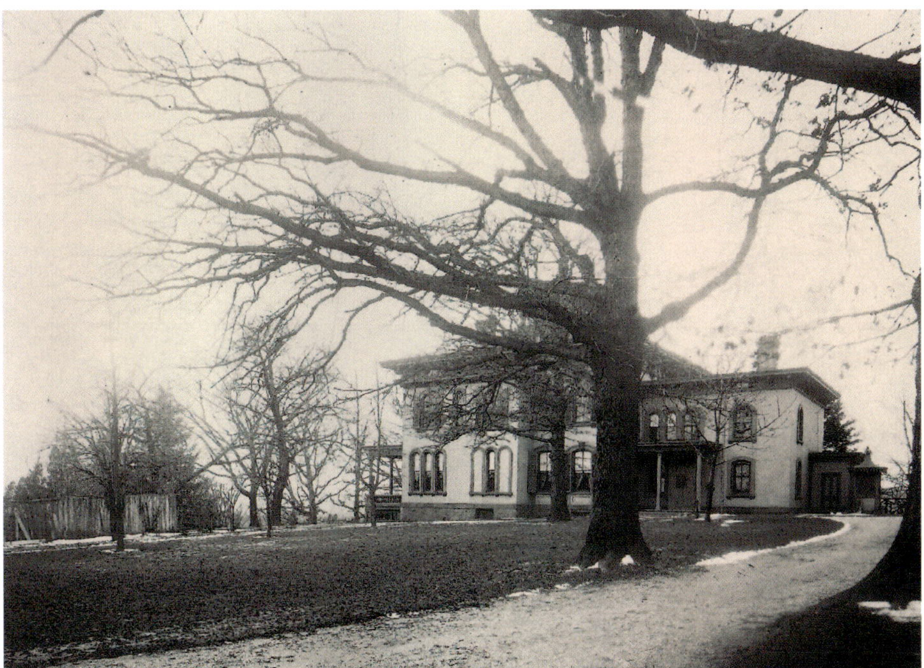

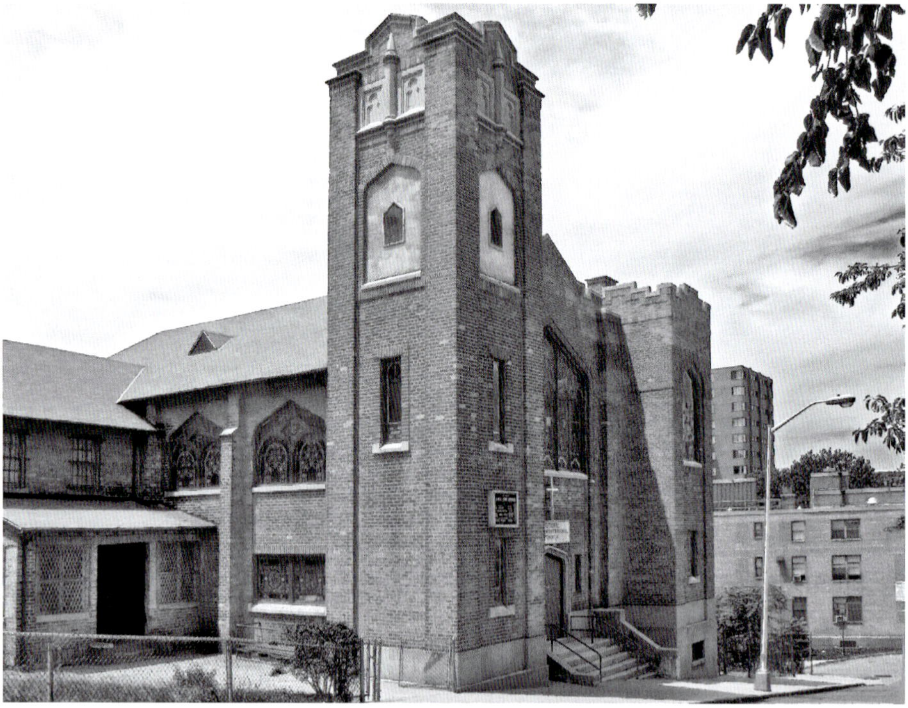

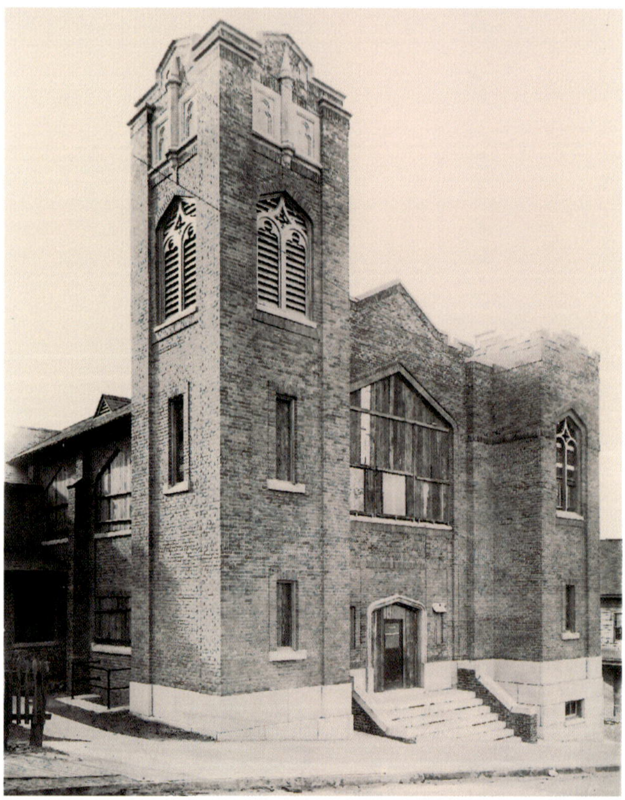

Institutional Africa Methodist Episcopal Zion Church was organized in 1871. The formal organization of the church was made with 10 members on the roll, with Rev. Jacob Thomas. Thomas was later made the reverend doctor of the New York Conference of the African Methodist Episcopal Zion Church. The church members worshipped in various halls around Yonkers until the board of trustees purchased a plot on Irving Place. In October 1922, ground was broken for a church building, which still stands on the site. (Courtesy Yonkers Historical Society.)

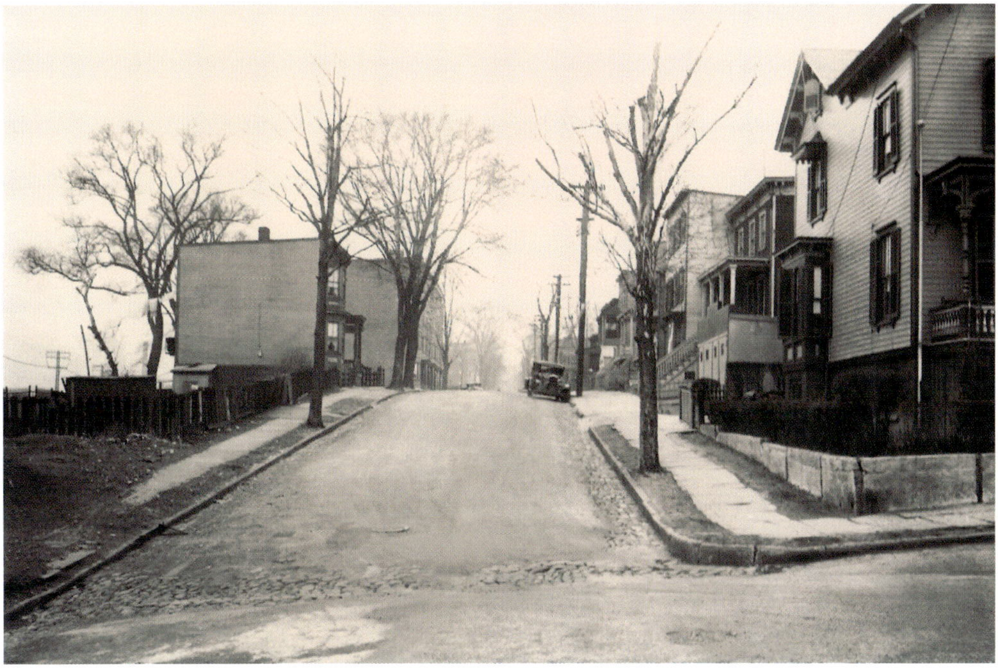

Beginning here at the corner of Lamartine Avenue and running to the north, Ravine Avenue was the street closest to the Hudson River in an area that was already densely built up in 1876. Thomas Fearon, one of the most renowned boat builders of the day, lived on Ravine Avenue near Point Street. He built his boats in a shop not far from his home. (Courtesy of Hudson River Museum.)

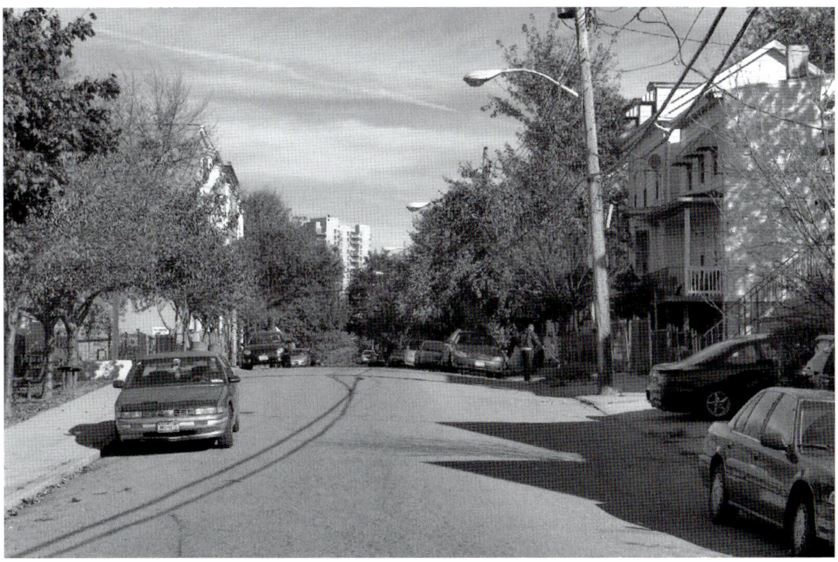

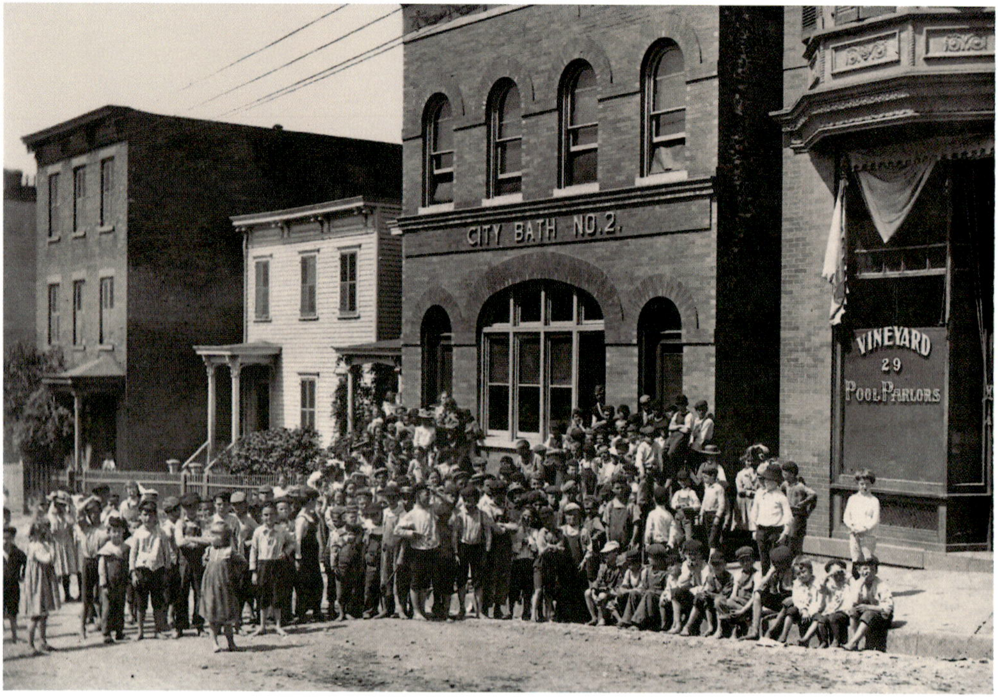

In 1896, the first municipally sponsored bathhouse in the state was built by the City of Yonkers in order to provide sanitary facilities. Public Bathhouse No. 2 was built in 1898. It was a rather small, two-story redbrick structure at 27 Vineyard Avenue. Remodeled in 1928, the bathhouse remained in service until 1962 when it was decommissioned by the city for economic reasons. Subsequently purchased by the Mount Hebron Apostolic Temple, the interior of the bathhouse was completely gutted to serve its new function as a church. (Courtesy of Hudson River Museum.)

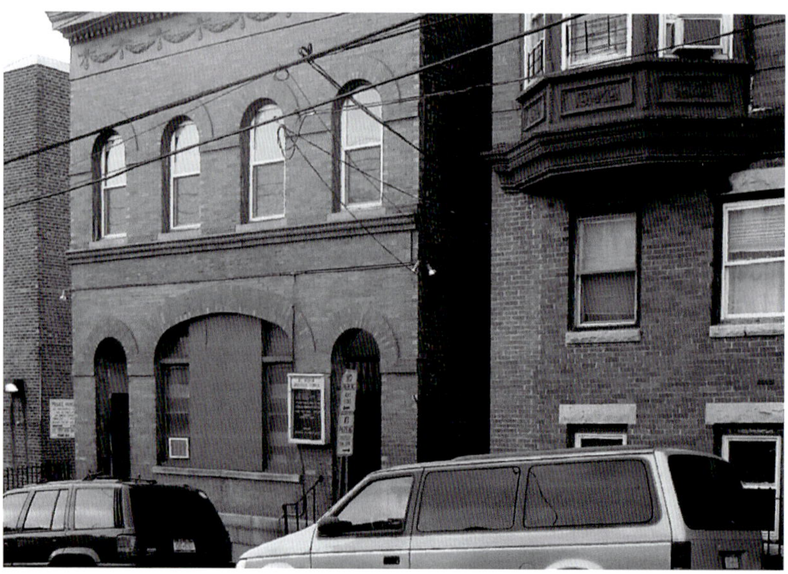

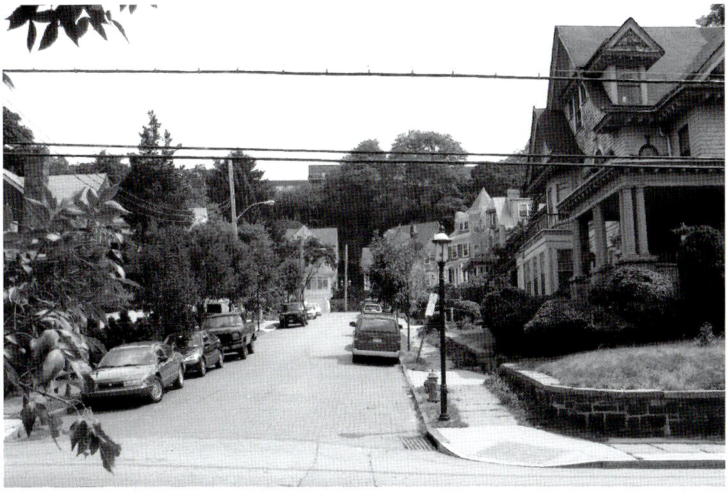

By the 1890s, Yonkers had become one of the largest cities in New York. Its growth was even further accelerated when electrified trolleys replace horsecars, starting in 1892. With easy access to the business center, many areas of open land at the edges of the city were subdivided and developed into new suburban neighborhoods. Among these was Halcyon Place, which includes 16 properties in northwest Yonkers dating from the mid-19th century to the early years of the 20th century. The area displays a broad range of styles, such as French Second Empire and Queen Anne. Halcyon Place became a Yonkers local landmark in June 1994. (Courtesy of Yonkers Planning Bureau.)

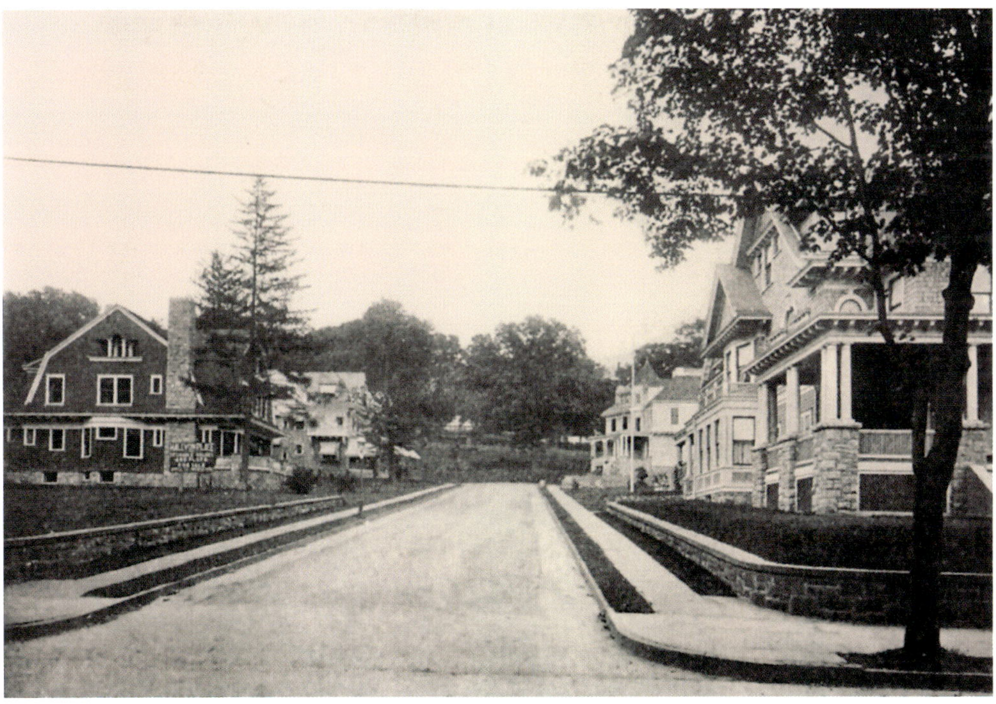

For many years, the generator of electric current for the New York Central Railroad, and later for the Consolidated Edison Company, was the huge Glenwood Power Plant on the Yonkers riverfront that stands idle today. It was bought by a private developer and plans are underway for renovation. (Courtesy of Robert Yasinsac.)

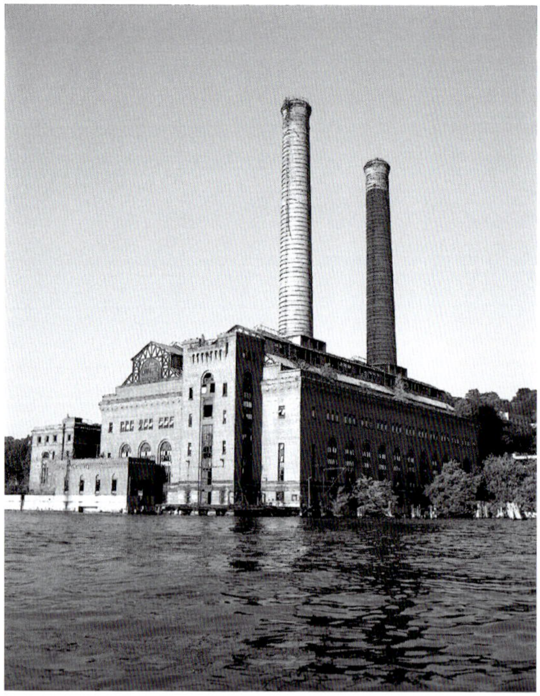

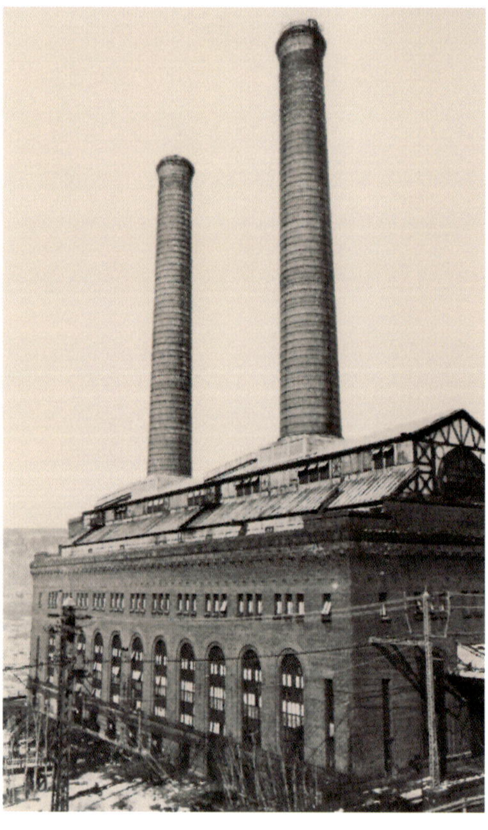

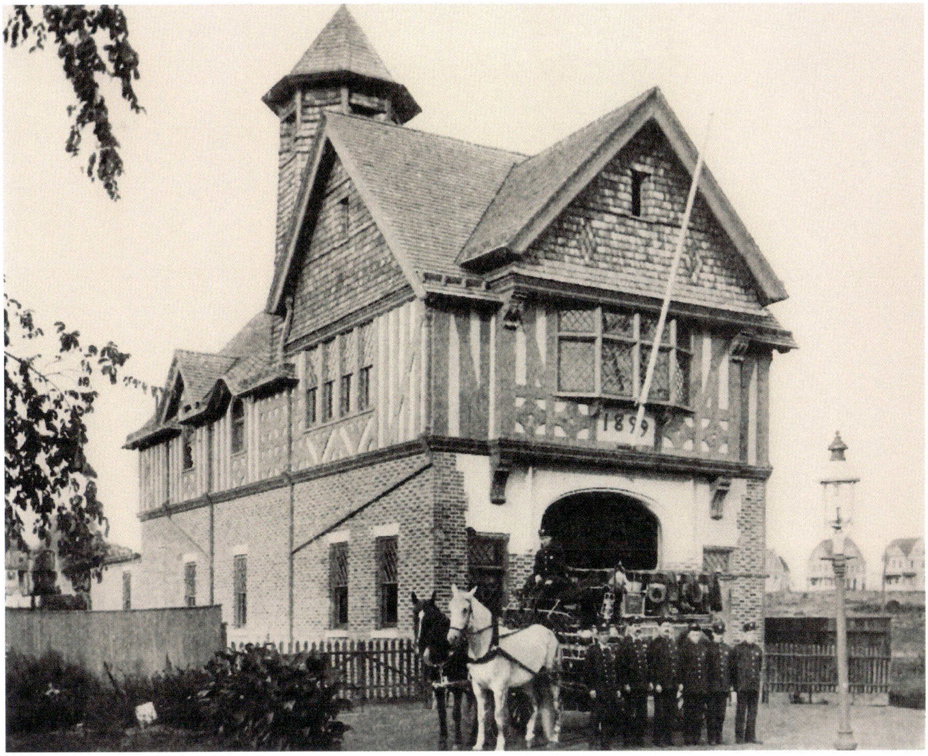

In 1901, Engine Company No. 5 on Shonnard Place went into commission. This firehouse was demolished and a second one built in 1931 at 53 Shonnard Place. In 1916, the fire department became 100 percent motorized, ending the era of the horse-drawn apparatus. The present firehouse is shared by the Yonkers Fire and Police Departments. (Courtesy of Don Kreutzberg.)

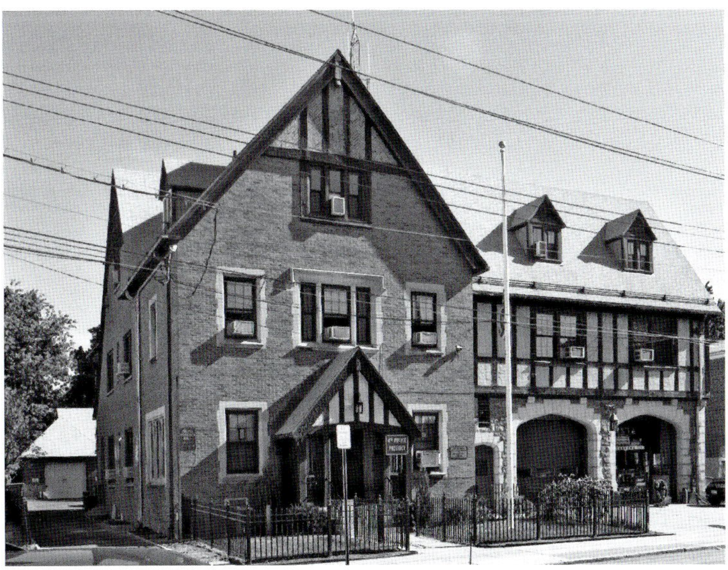

Glenview Mansion, built in 1876 by John Bond Trevor, is an important and treasured landmark in Yonkers. In 1922, after the death of Trevor's widow, the City of Yonkers purchased the Trevor estate in order to preserve the mansion and surrounding lands as a park. It became the Museum of Science and Art. Renamed the Hudson River Museum in 1948, a modern museum was built in front of the house in the late 1960s. The house has been restored to the way it was when lived in by the Trevors. (Courtesy of Yonkers Historical Society.)

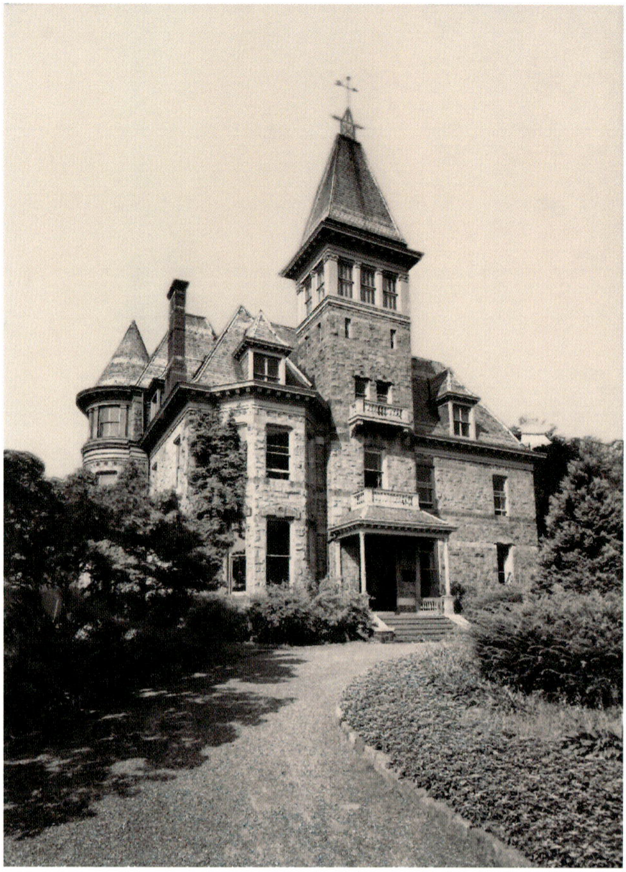

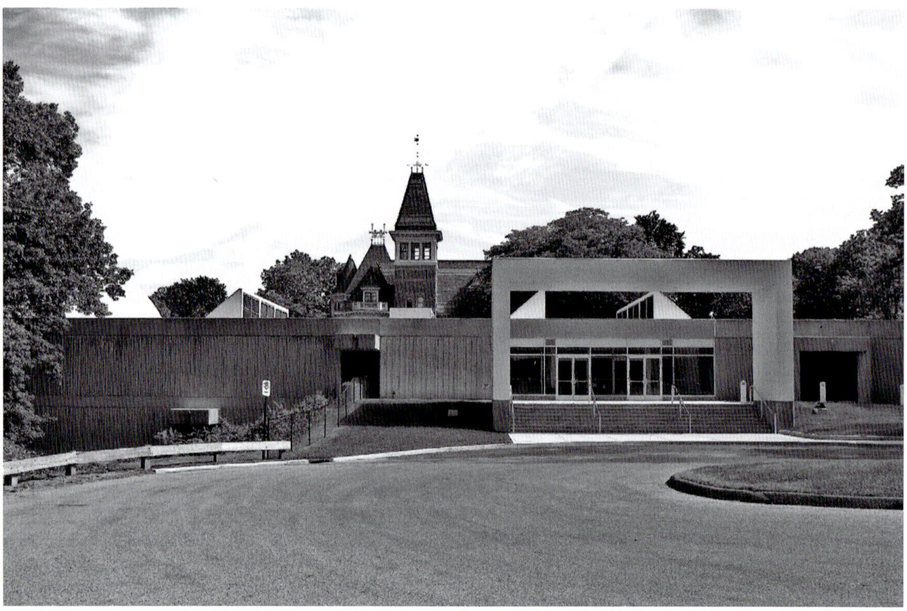

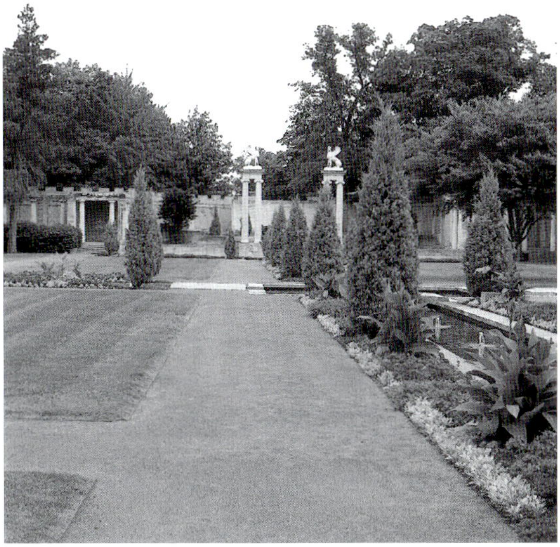

Untermyer Gardens on Broadway in North Yonkers was once part of the 111-acre estate of Samuel Untermyer, a self-made millionaire and internationally known lawyer. He developed the then nationally known Grecian Gardens with classic Beaux-Arts landscaping, one of a few ever completed in America. It has some 10,000 square feet of exterior mosaic, foundations, a reflecting pool, and canals that mirror the water motif of the Hudson River. (Courtesy of Yonkers Historical Society.)

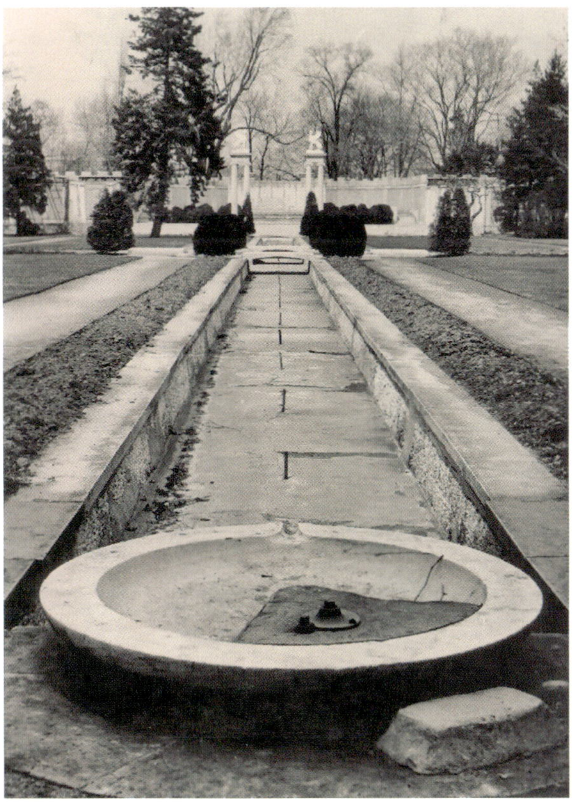

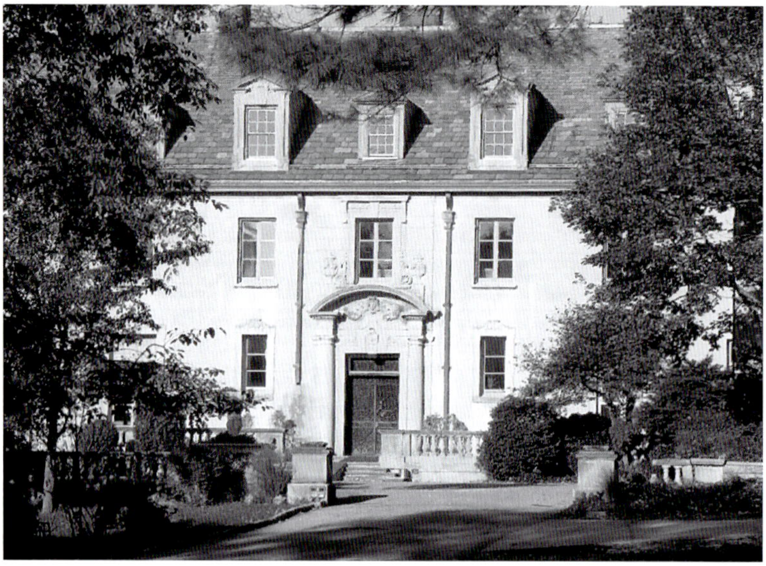

Alder Manor, an Italian Renaissance Revival mansion completed in 1912, was designed by the noted architectural firm of Carriere and Hastings of New York City. The inspiration for this magnificent structure came from William Boyce Thompson (1869–1930), who rose from obscure origins as the son of a carpenter from Alder Gulch, Montana, to become one of the leading financial advisors of some of the wealthiest patrons of New York's early 20th century. The mansion is presently under restoration by its current owners, Tara Circle, an Irish cultural organization. (Courtesy of Yonkers Historical Society.)

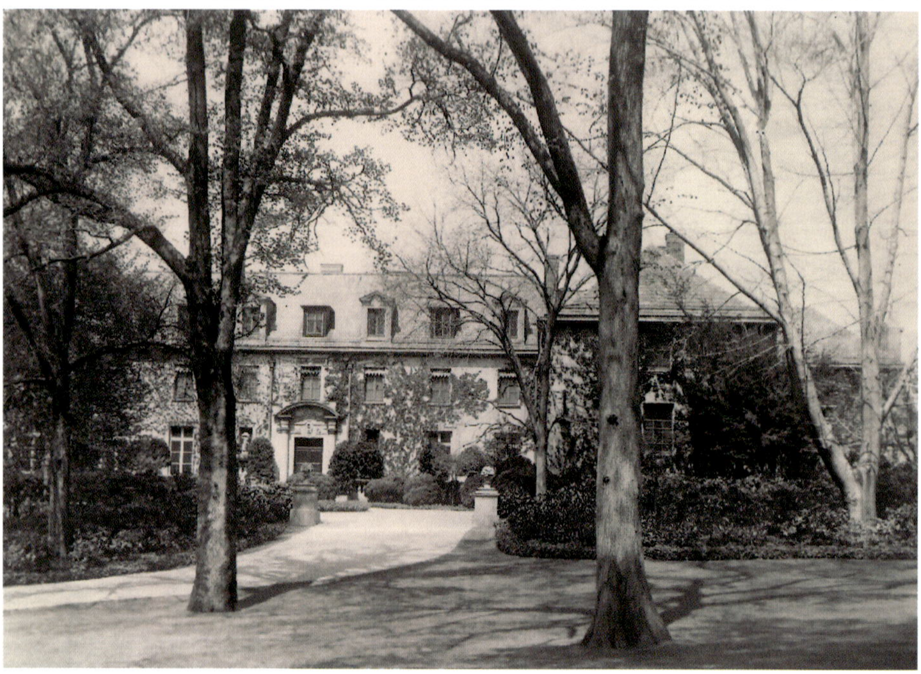

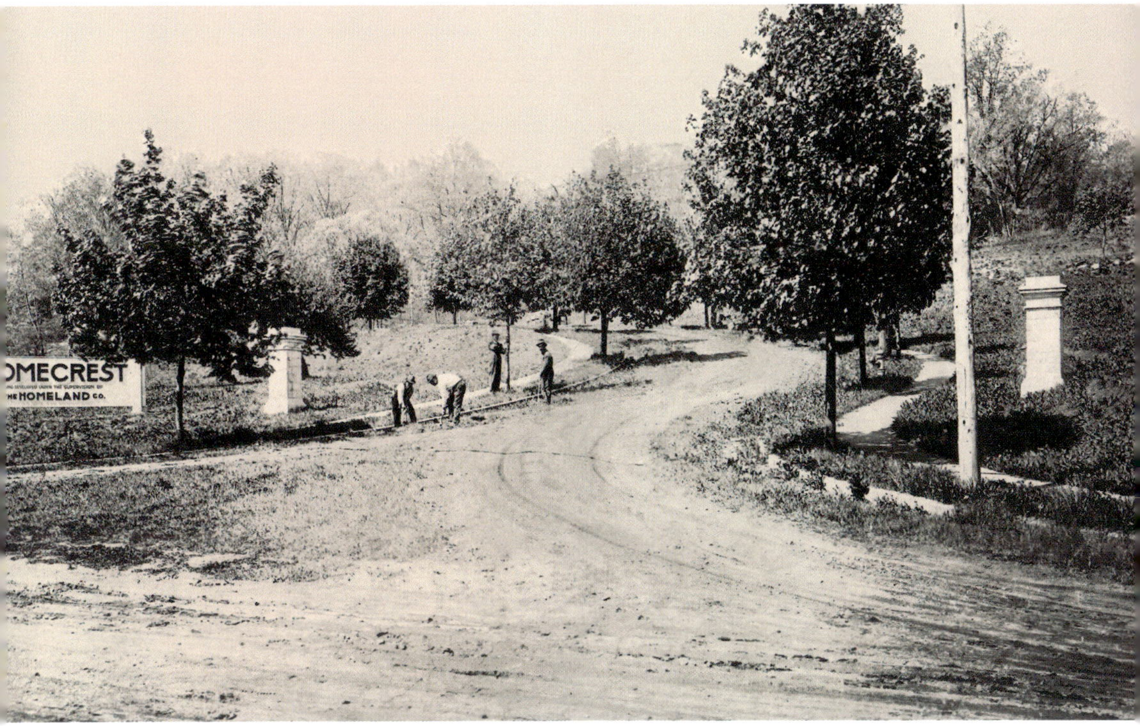

Homecrest was the first community to be opened up by the Homeland Company, a real estate developer with offices on Main Street in Getty Square in the 1920s. The area's main entrance is at the corner of Nepperhan and Cross Hill Avenues and is "located in a shaded hillside directly facing and adjoining Saw Mill River Parkway a few minutes from Getty Square on the No. 5 trolley," as advertised in 1925 in the *Yonkers Herald*. (Courtesy of Yonkers Historical Society.)

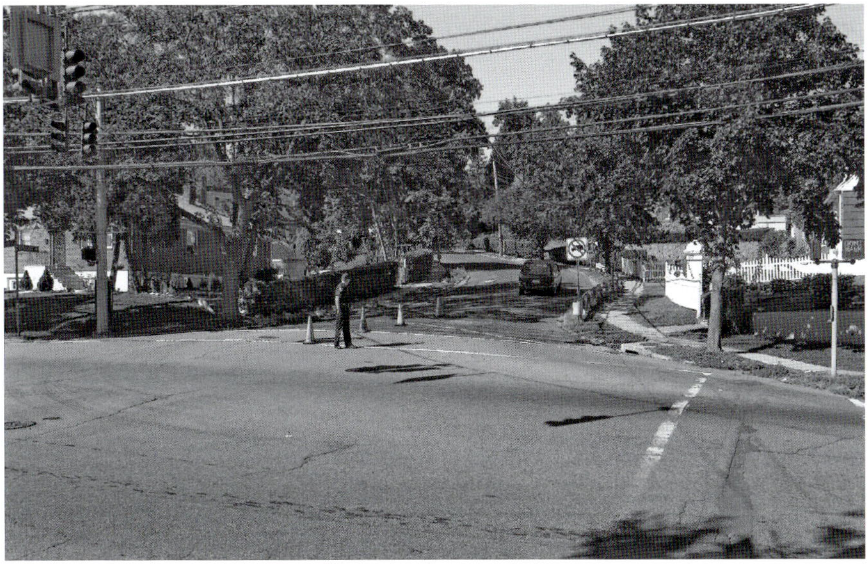

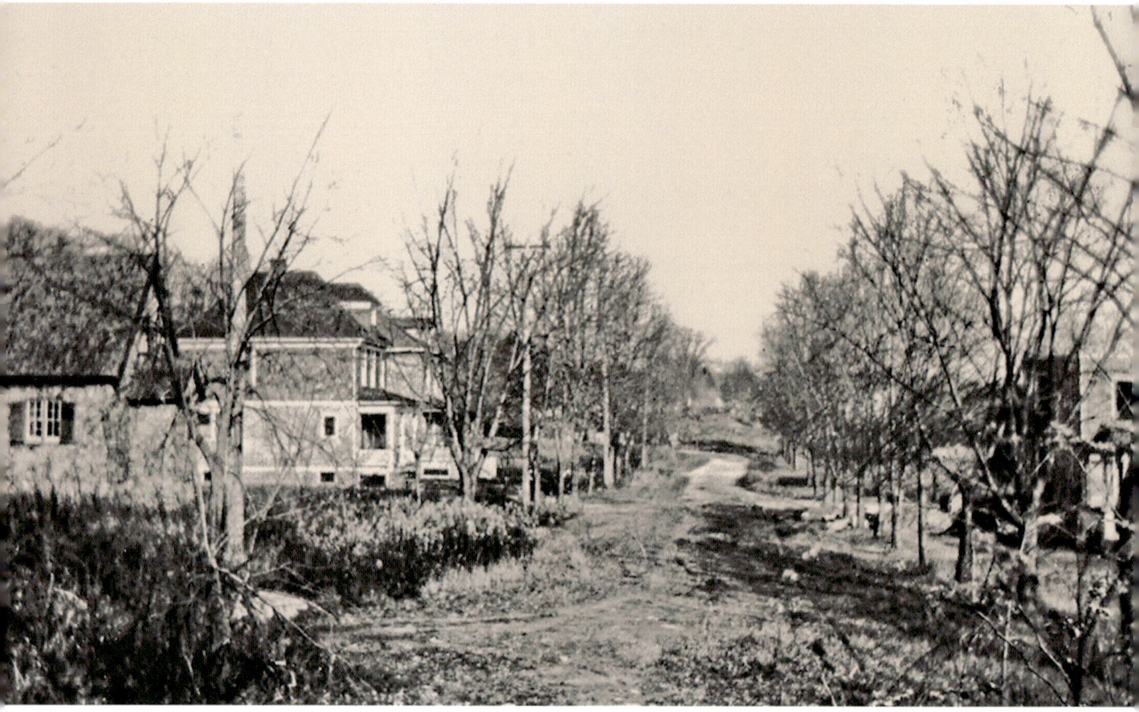

Looking at Truman Avenue north in this photograph, one can see old St. Mark's church in the left-hand corner. It had been demolished and a new one built on Nepperhan Avenue. At the top left is where St. Joseph's Cemetery begins. (Courtesy of Nepera Park Civic Association.)

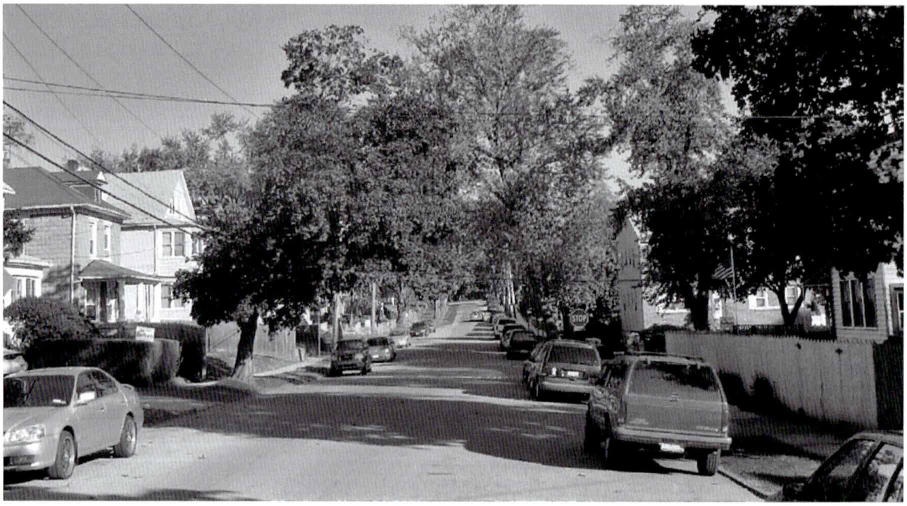

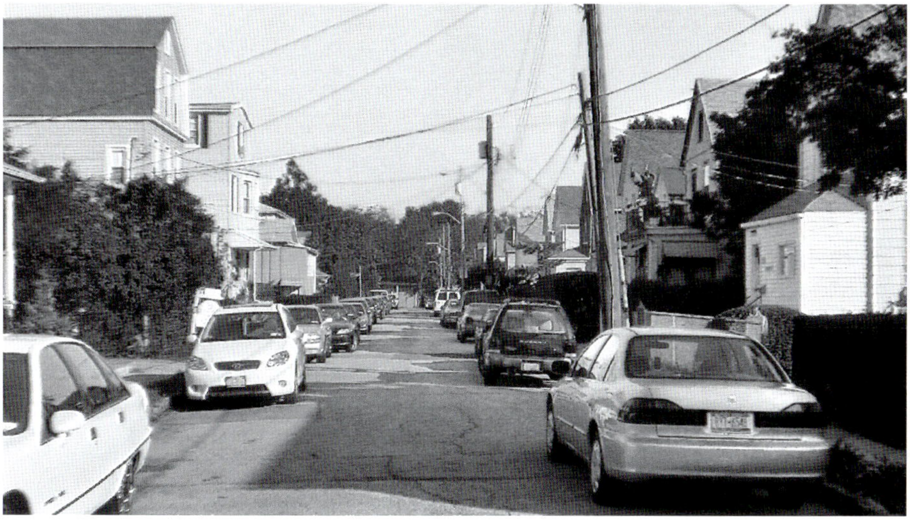

Marion Avenue was the beginning of a development one block east of Railroad Avenue where the Saw Mill River Parkway and the river separate Nepera Park. One of the original developments in Nepera Park, it was on property bought by Civil War veteran Col. James C. Truman in 1884. (Courtesy of Nepera Park Civic Association.)

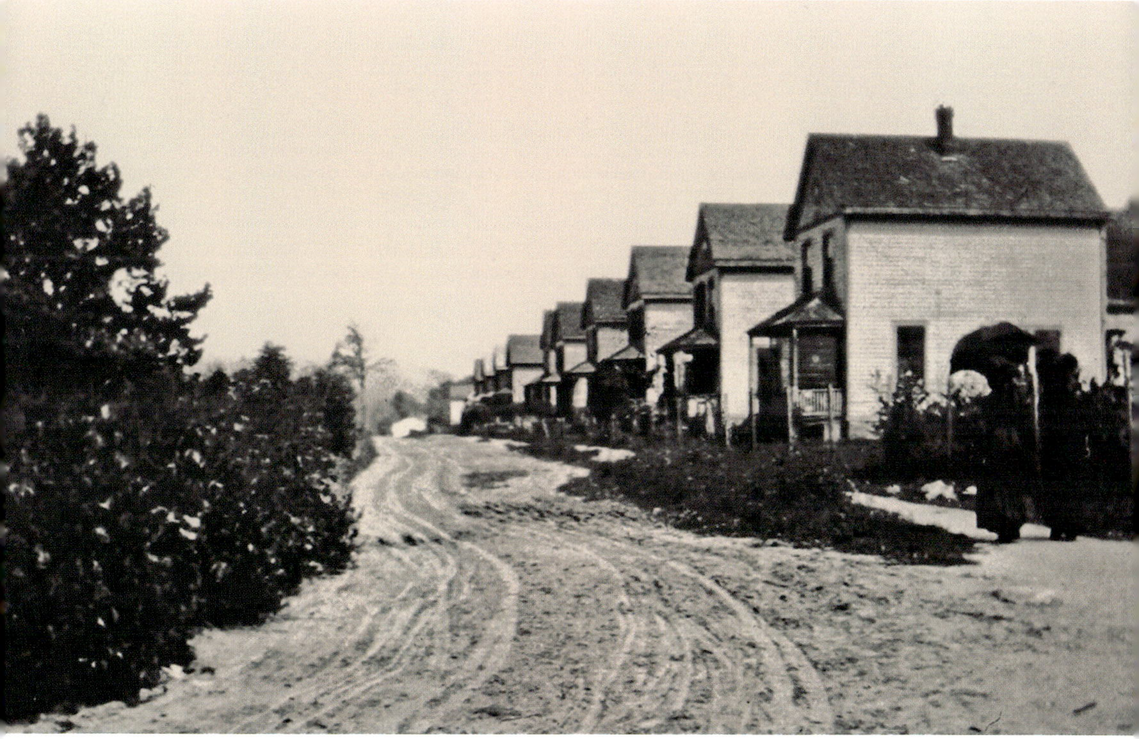

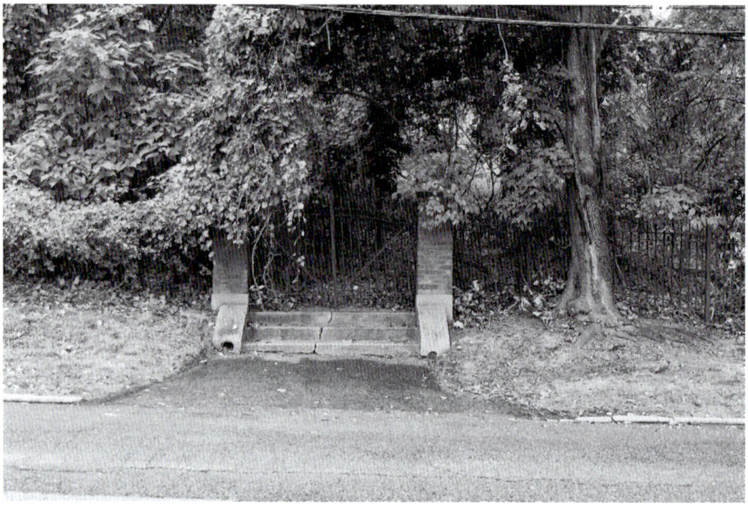

When William Boyce Thompson and Caleb C. Dula took over the Saegkill Golf Club in 1915, then located in the Nepperhan Valley, they changed the name to the Hudson River Country Club. The Hudson River Country Club purchased the estate of Eugene Clark, president of the Alexander Smith Carpet Company, located on the northeast corner of North Broadway and Odell Avenue in 1919. Included in the purchase was a 128-acre parcel north of the property that was converted into a standard 18-hole golf course. The property is now the site of the Southern Westchester Executive Park. (Courtesy of Yonkers Planning Bureau.)

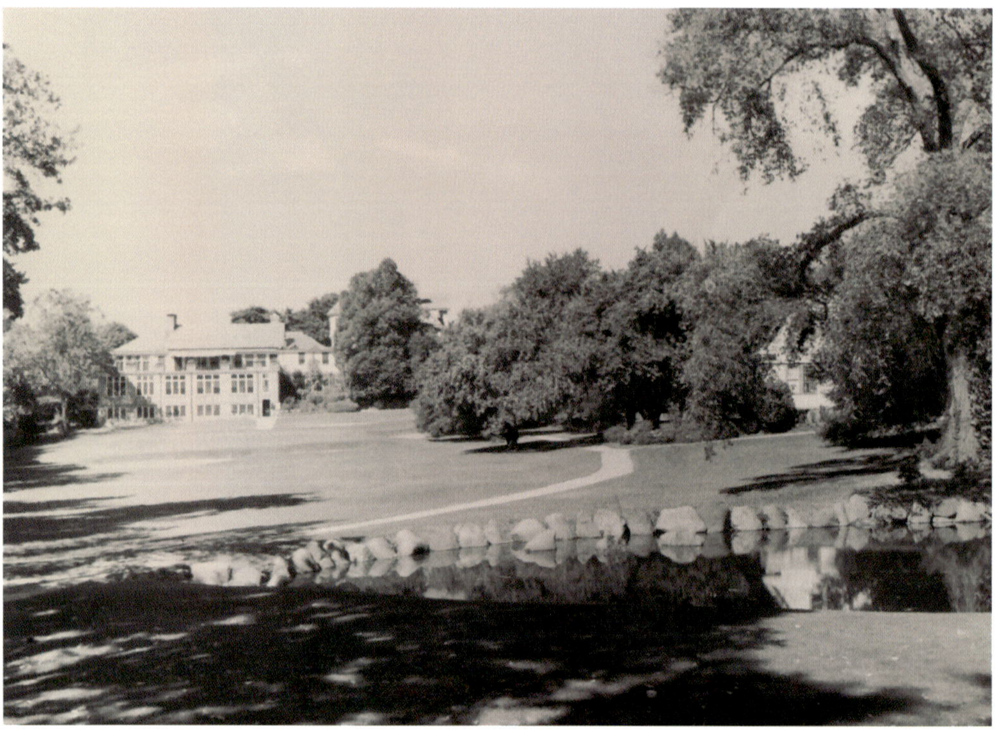

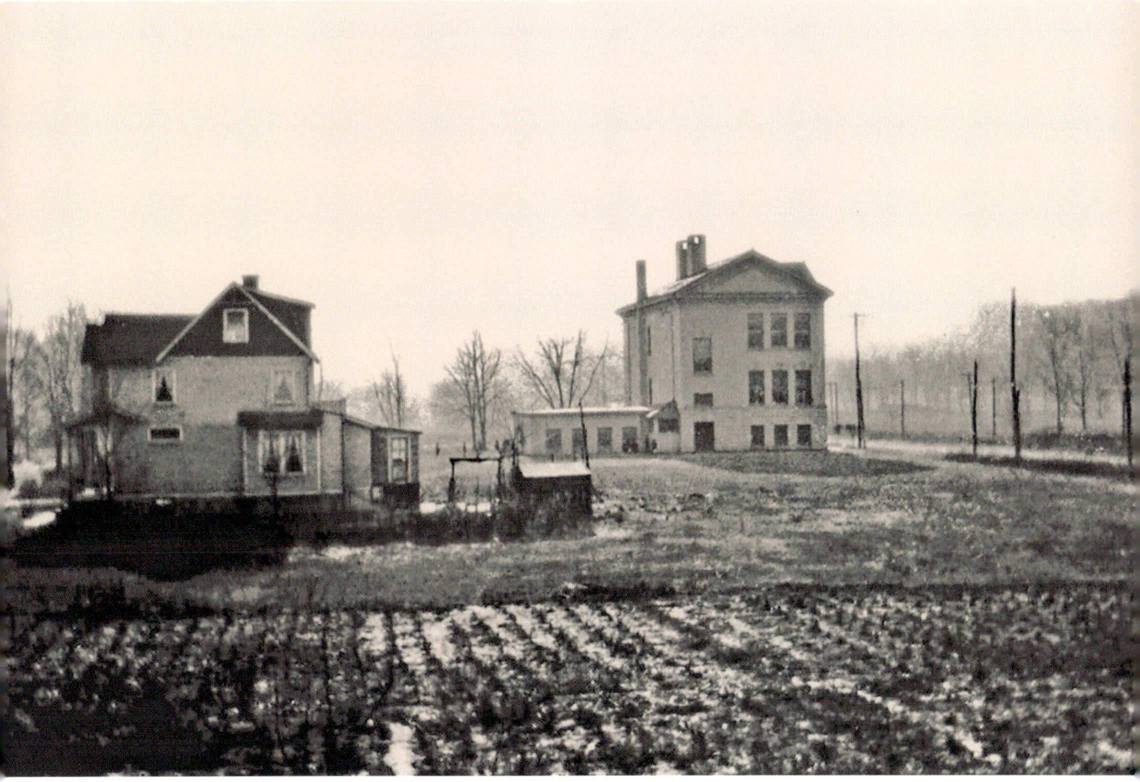

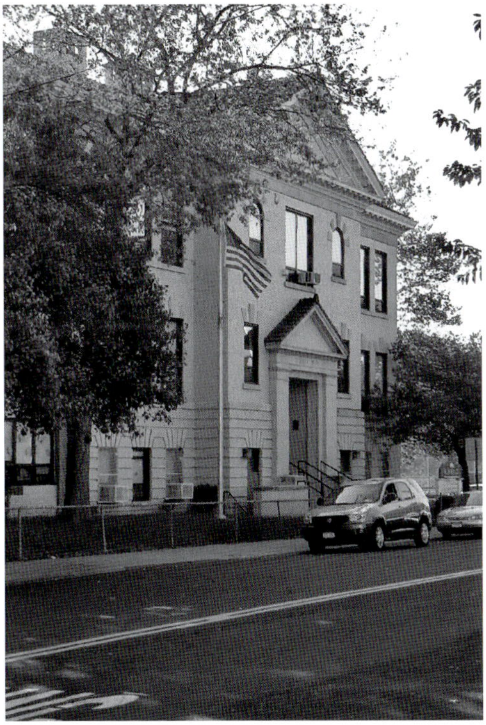

Located at Nepperhan Avenue and Reade Street, Public School 22 was constructed in 1912. At that time, there were only four classrooms in the building, not counting a room in the basement that was used as an assembly room. As the Homecrest and Homefield neighborhoods grew in the years during and after World War I, so too did the need for more classroom space. A sizeable addition to school 22, therefore, was built in 1924. Having long served as a junior high school, the school currently provides instruction for students from prekindergarten through fifth grade. (Courtesy of Nepera Park Civic Association.)

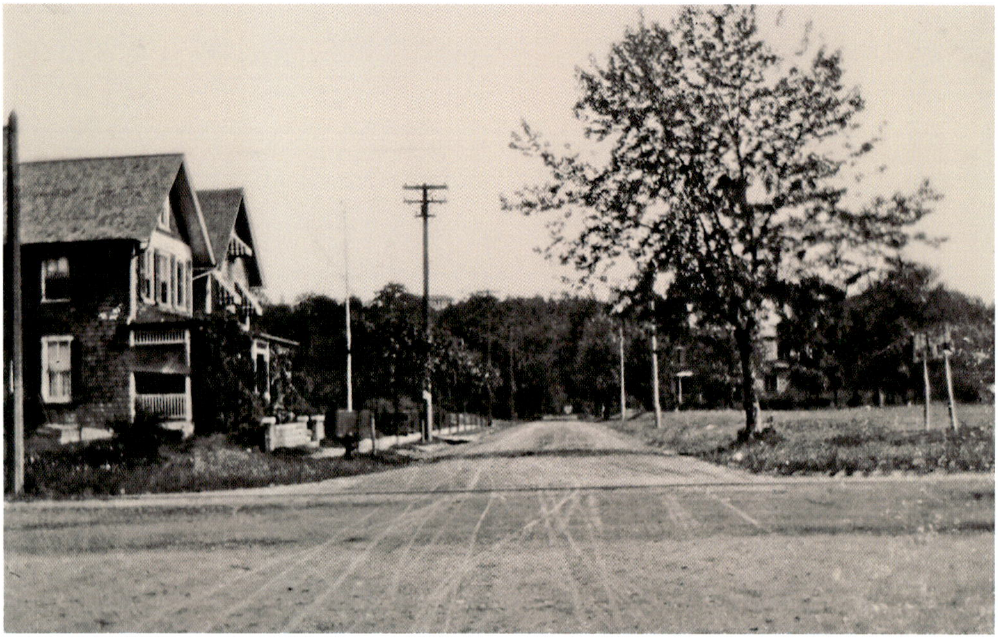

Nepera Park was the home of the Nepera Native American tribe, who pitched their wigwams on the flatlands and hills along the Saw Mill River. Many early moving pictures were filmed there, including *The Last of the Mohicans*. Nepera Park was originally founded by Col. James C. Truman.

Heart Street was the center of Nepera Park. The stores shown in the photograph at Hearst Street and Nepperhan Avenue were originally a delicatessen, a barbershop, a shoemaker, and a bicycle shop. There were two apartments above the stores. (Courtesy of Nepera Park Civic Association.)

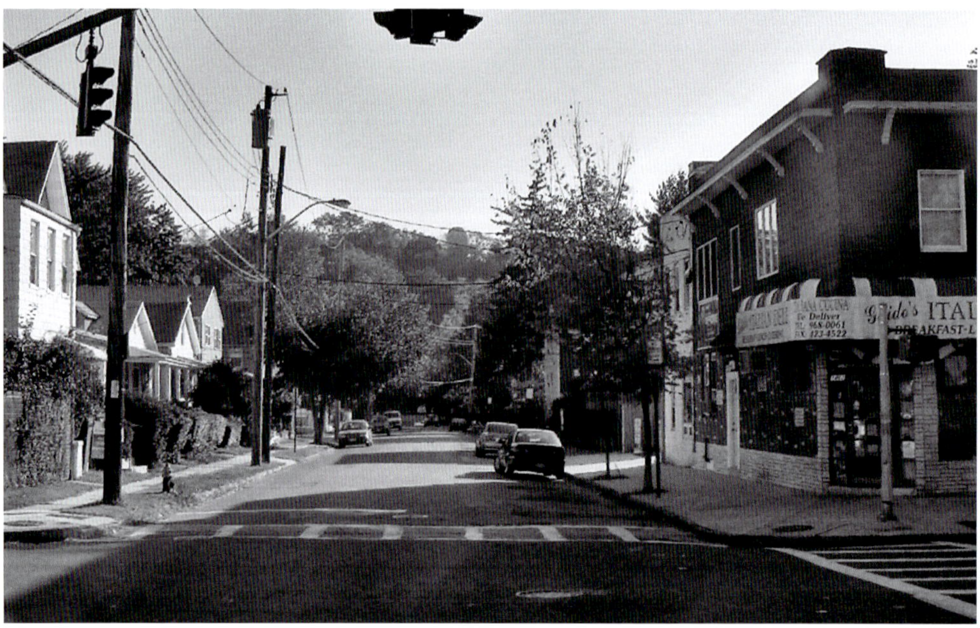

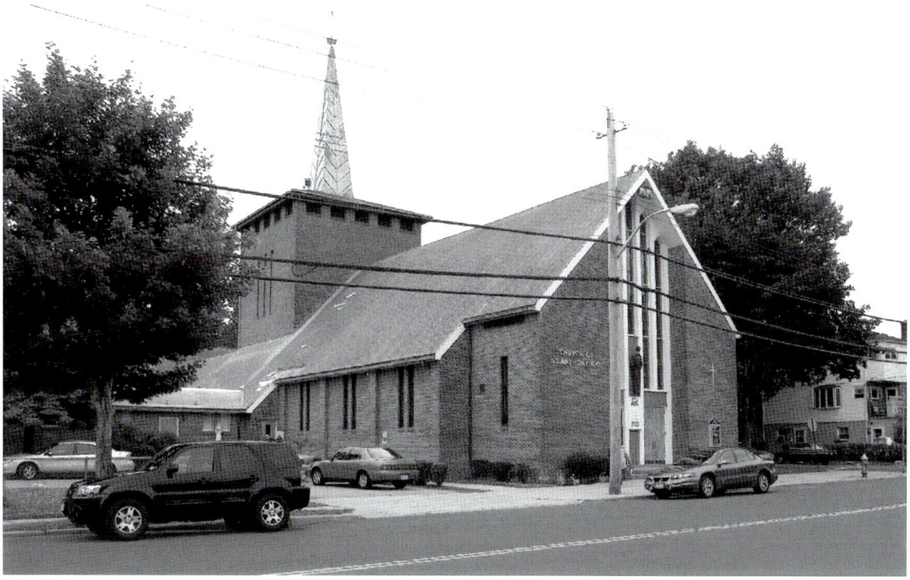

St. Anthony's church was originally on the corner of Hearst Street and Nepperhan Avenue. In 1934, on adjacent property owned by the church, a new hall was built and the church moved to the site. This church burned down in 1951. The parish used the Colts Club to hold mass while a new church, hall, rectory, and school were being built in 1952 on the corner of Nepperhan Avenue and Squire Place. (Courtesy of Nepera Park Civic Association.)

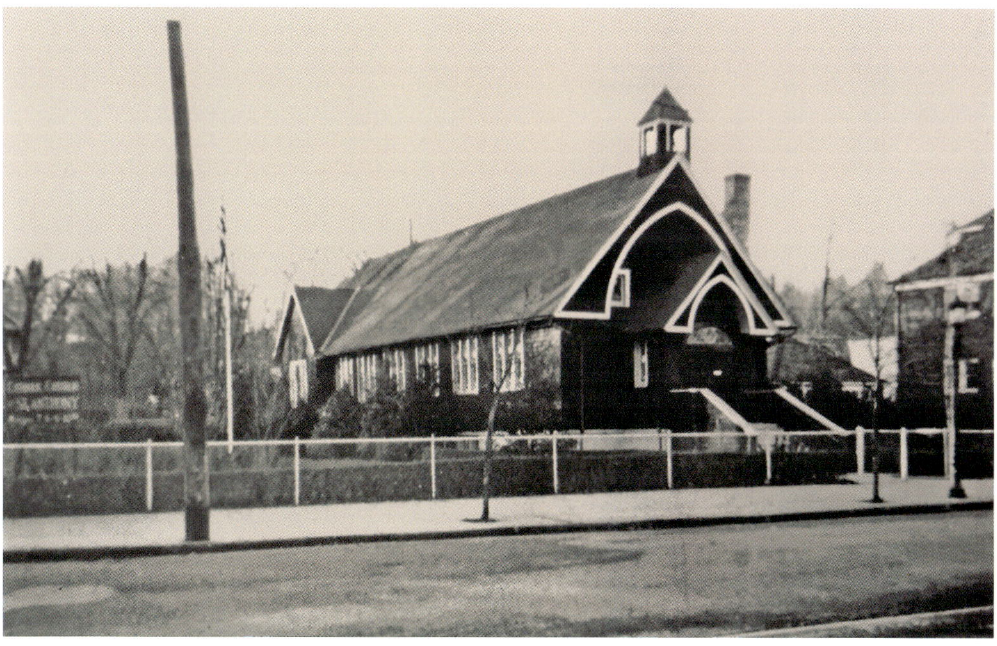

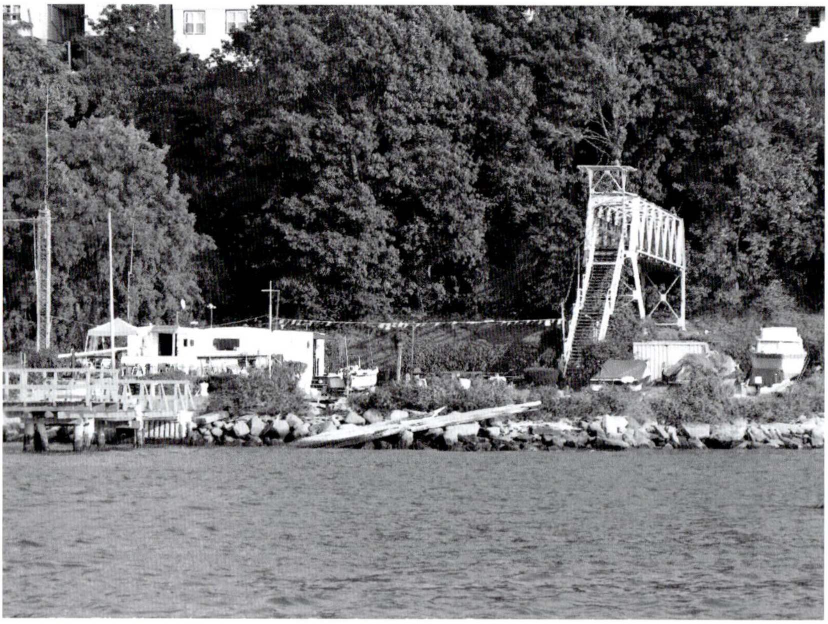

Organized in 1889, the Corinthian Yacht Club was built when it acquired property at the foot of Vark Street. The club celebrated Independence Day with rowing, swimming, and tub races. In the evening, lights, lanterns, and fireworks were displayed. The club was moved and is presently located at 771 Warburton Avenue. (Courtesy of Yonkers Historical Society.)

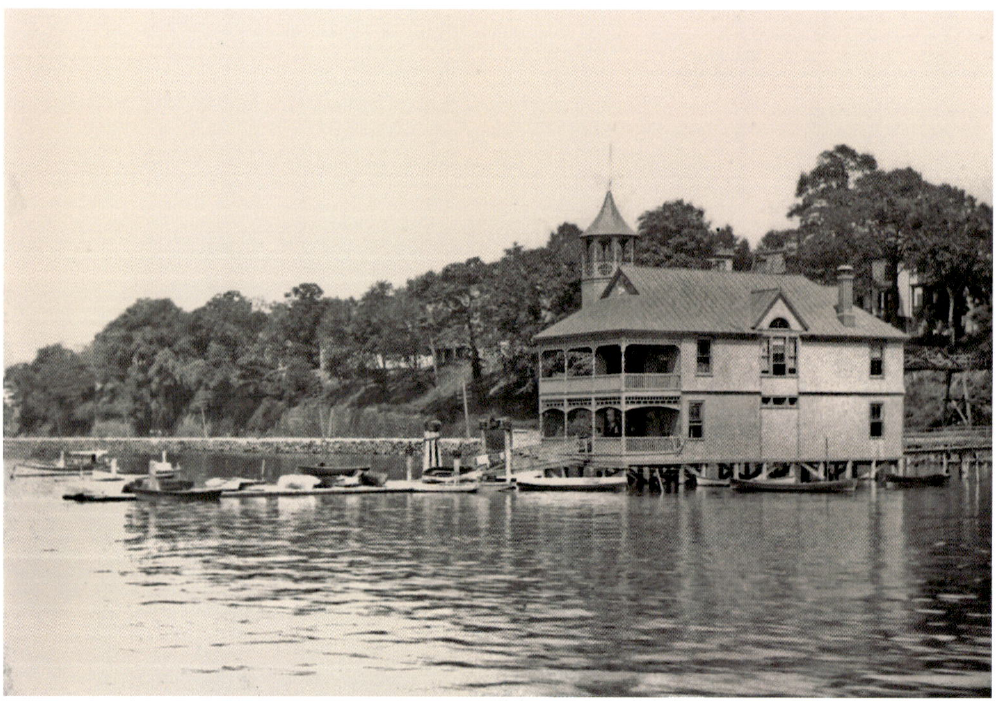

CHAPTER

NEPPERHAN VALLEY

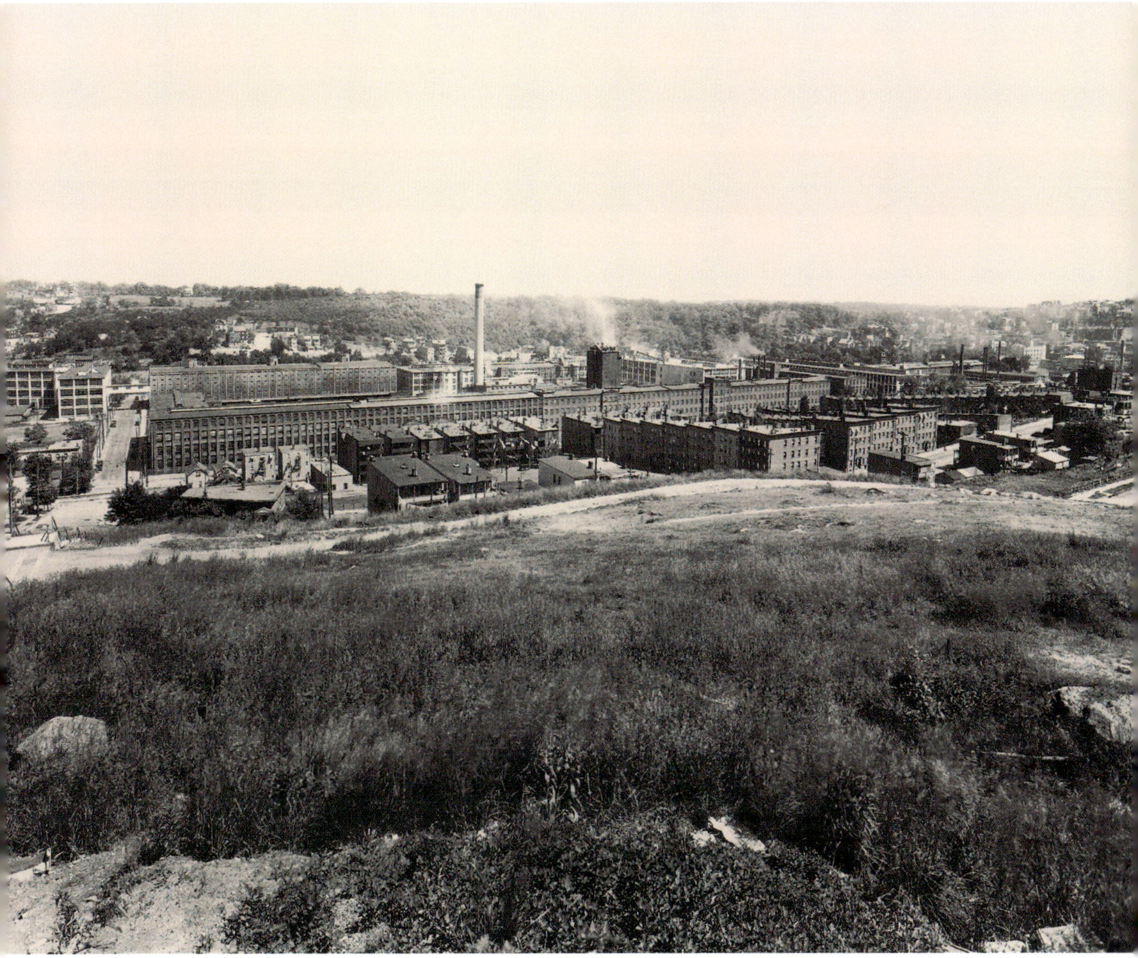

Alexander Smith Carpet Mills first opened in Yonkers in 1864, and at the height of production in the 1940s, it employed over 7,000 workers. Revolutionizing carpet manufacturing with the development of new technology, the mills achieved worldwide recognition. The carpet mills had a history of opposition to organized labor and announced their closing during a strike in 1954, laying off 5,000 workers. (Courtesy of Yonkers Historical Society.)

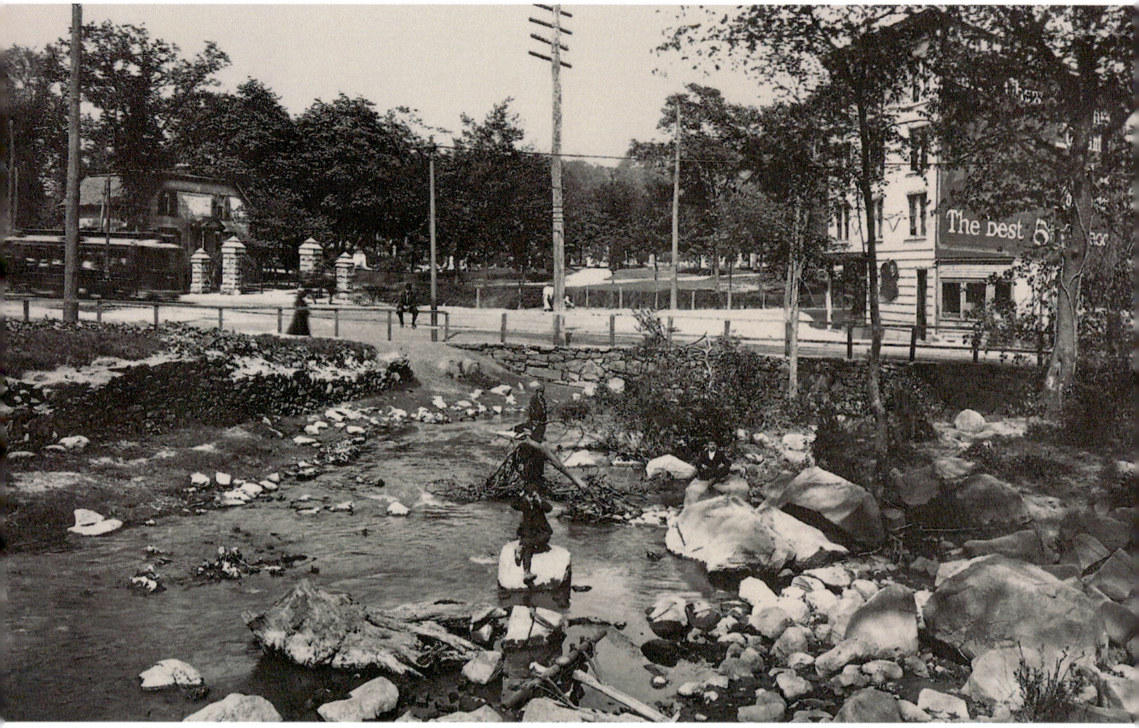

Oakland Cemetery was established on December 6, 1866. Located on the corner of Saw Mill River Road and Ashburton Avenue, it forms a portion of the Nepperhan Valley. The cemetery is entered through impressive iron gates that were originally constructed in 1867 and renovated in 1905. Many well-known Yonkers families have plots in the cemetery. This includes Dr. Charles A. Leale, the surgeon who first reached Pres. Abraham Lincoln's side when he was shot at Ford's Theater in Washington, D.C. (Courtesy of Hudson River Museum.)

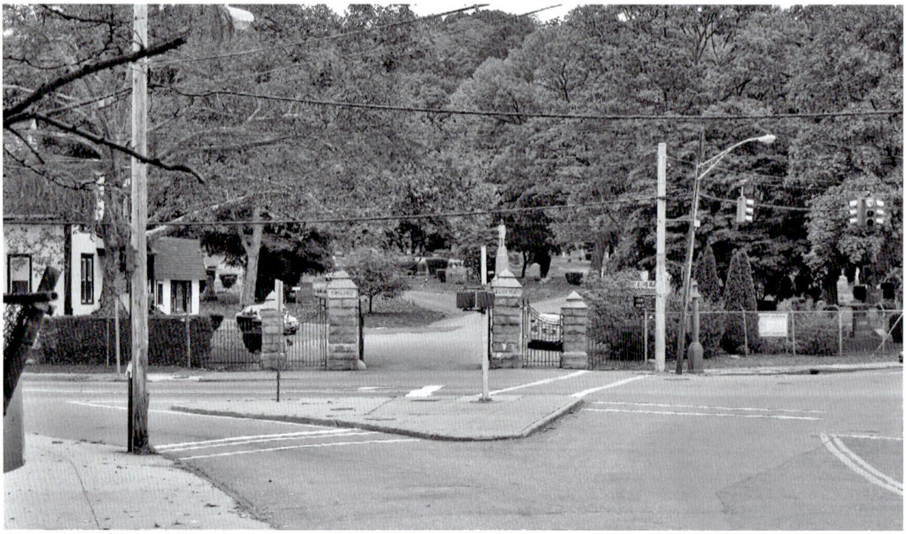

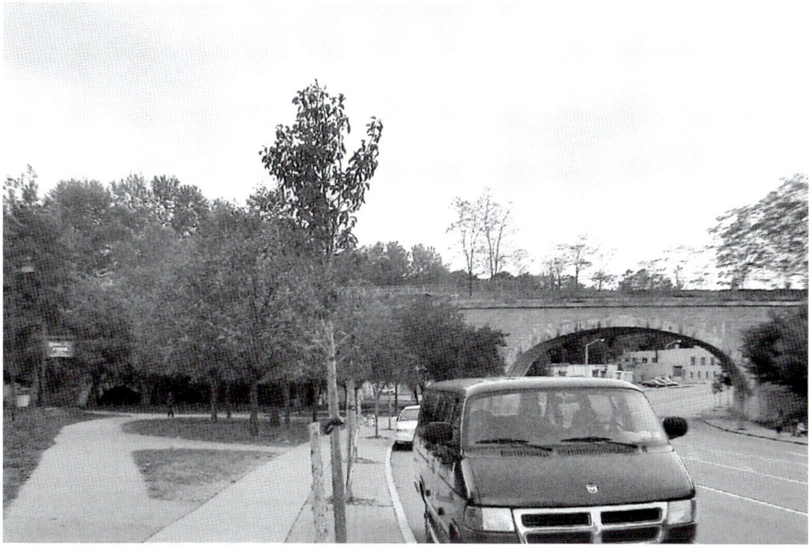

The Old Croton Aqueduct was built in response to the cholera and typhoid epidemics and uncontrollable fires that repeatedly devastated New York City due to its inadequate water supply. Construction began in 1837 and was carried out primarily by a workforce of Irish immigrant laborers. From 1842 to 1955, millions of gallons of water rushed through the brick and stone conduit. The entire length is known today as the Old Croton Aqueduct Trailway. As the trailway veers southeast over the Nepperhan Avenue Arterial and the Saw Mill River then across Walnut Street and Yonkers Avenue, it becomes virtually indistinguishable from city streets. (Courtesy of Hon. Nicholas Spano.)

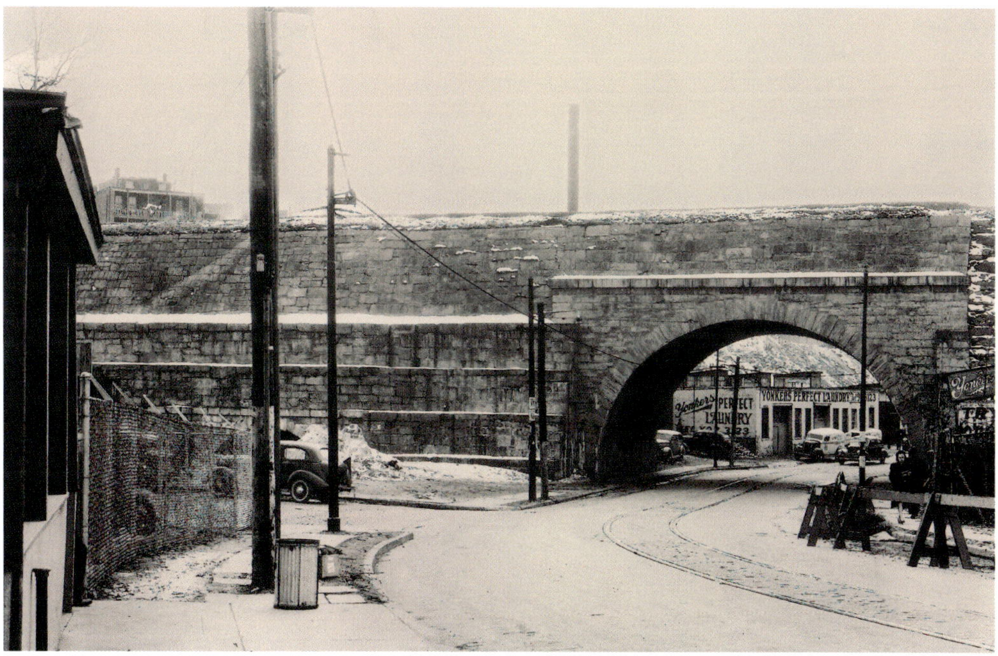

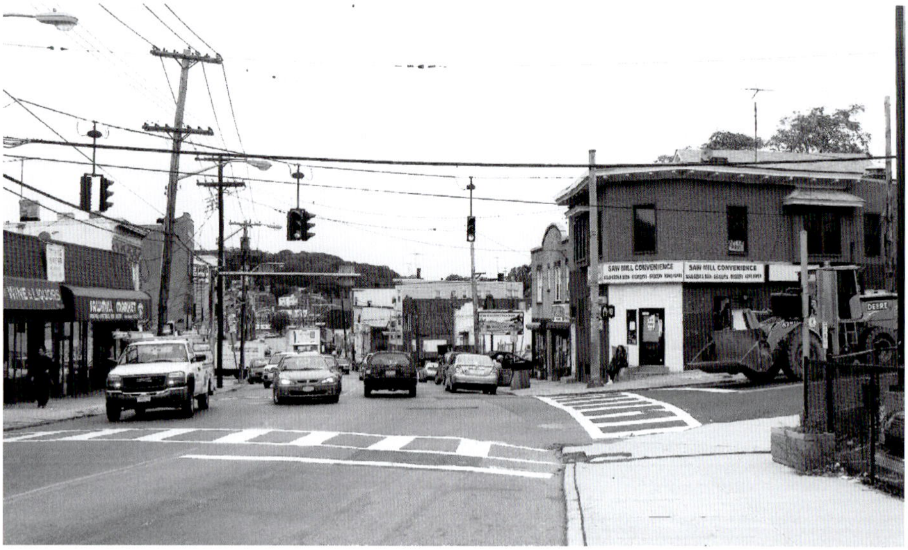

The intersection of Saw Mill River Road and Lockwood Avenue serves as one of the centers for the commercial development on the east side of the Saw Mill River in the Nepperhan Valley. Lockwood Avenue, lined with shops and businesses, extends from this point east through the Nepperhan Heights and Bryn Mawr neighborhoods to Mile Square Road. (Courtesy of Hudson River Museum.)

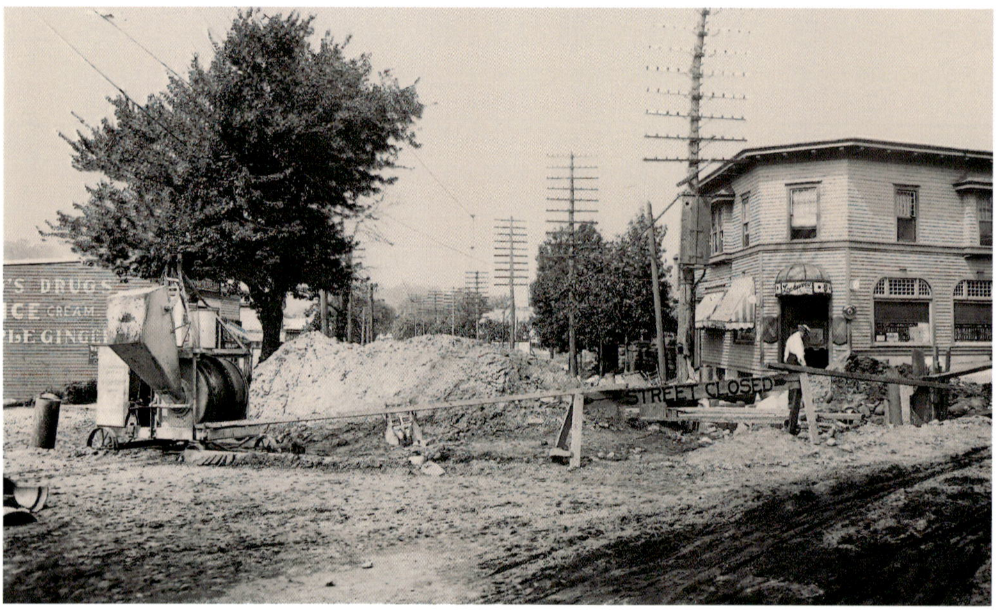

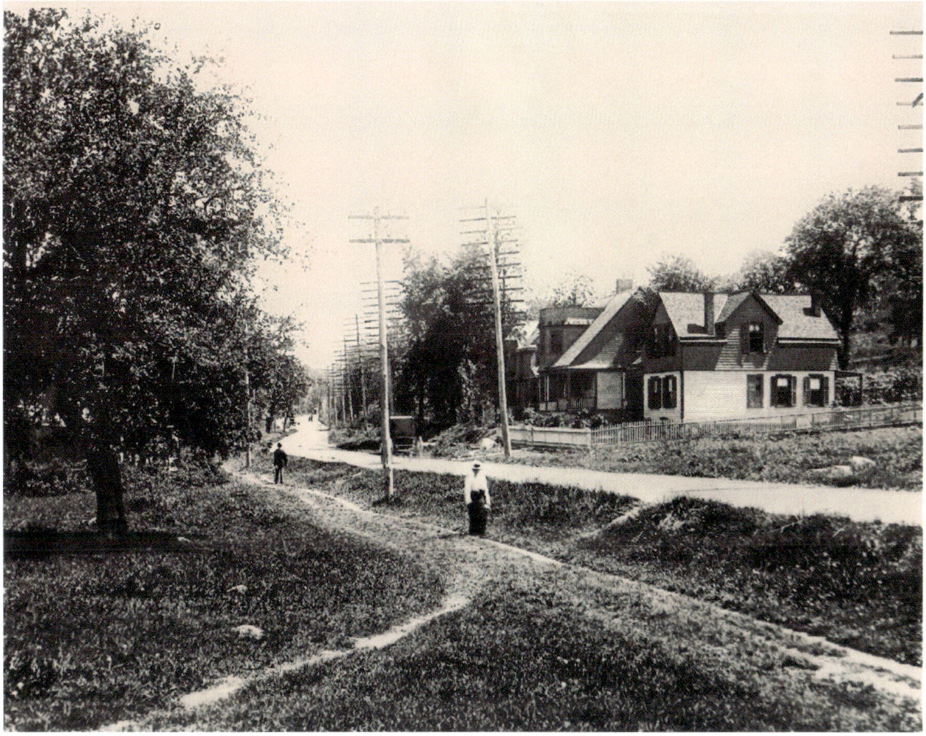

As Yonkers's major thoroughfare nearest to the Saw Mill River's eastern bank, Saw Mill River Road has always served as both a gateway to the industries along the eastern bank of the Saw Mill River and also an access point to the residential areas that rise along the eastern side of the Nepperhan Valley. With today's greater density of development along Saw Mill River Road, the dual nature of land uses along the road is quite apparent. (Courtesy of Yonkers Historical Society.)

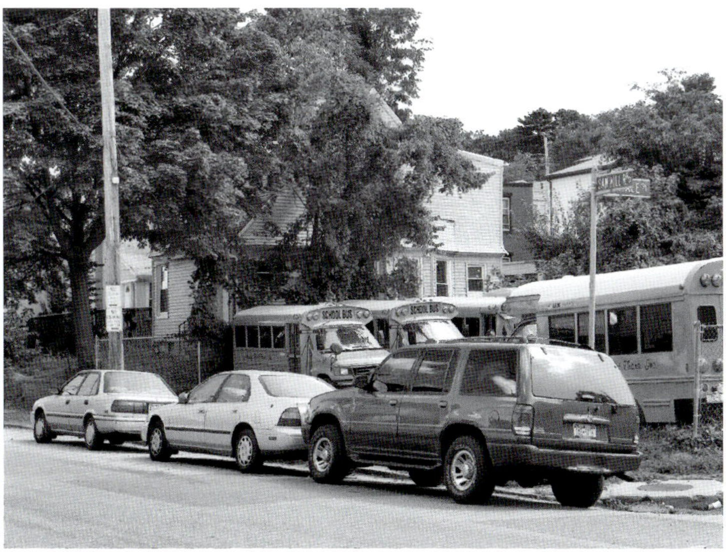

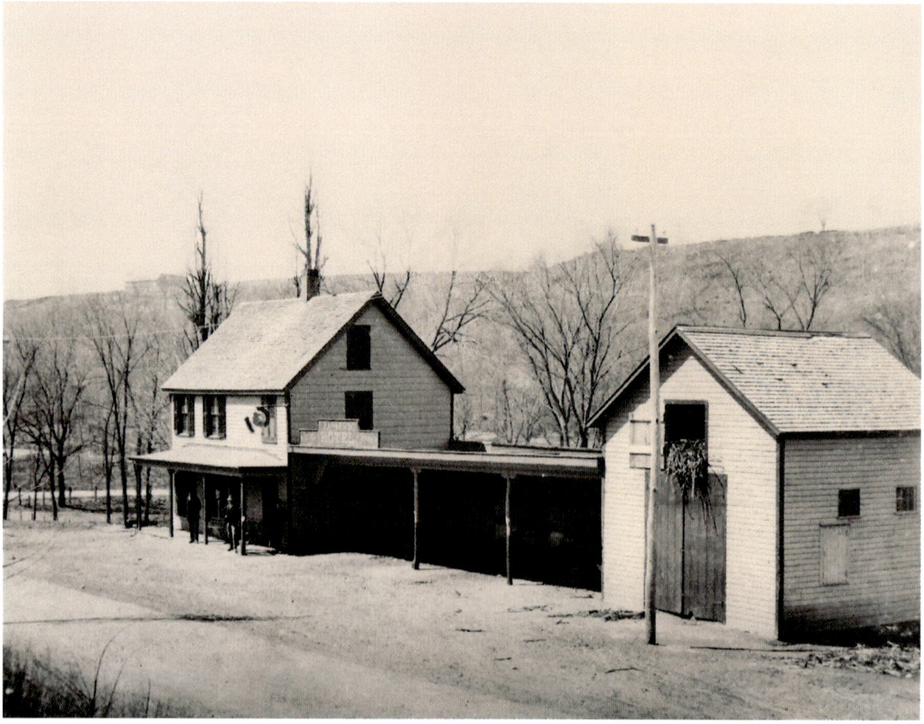

Fishers Grove was a popular picnic area and beer garden that Yonkers working people could reach by taking the No. 5 trolley, which ran on Nepperhan Avenue beginning at the foot of Main Street. As industrial Yonkers progressed Phelps Dodge built its copper wiring plant on the site. In later years Liberty Lines Bus took over the site as its main depot. (Courtesy of Donald Kreutzberg.)

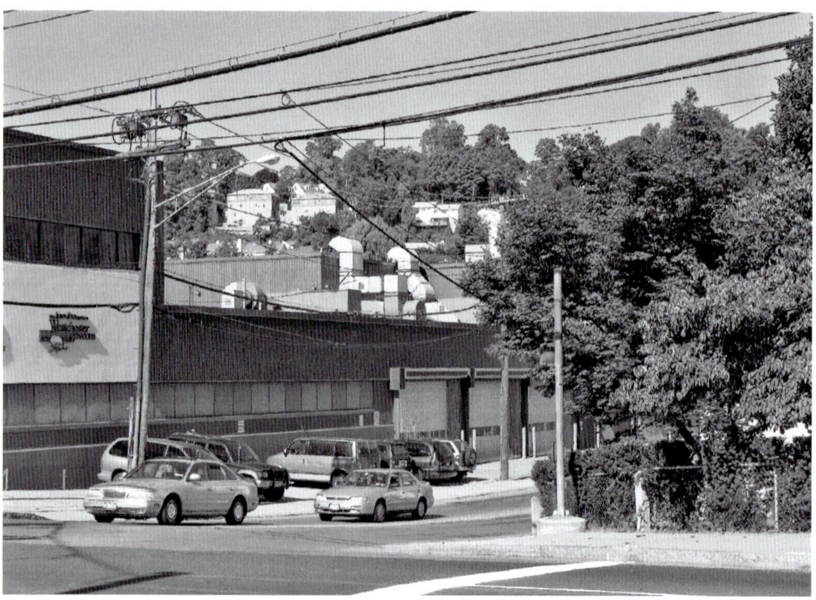

CHAPTER

NORTHEAST YONKERS

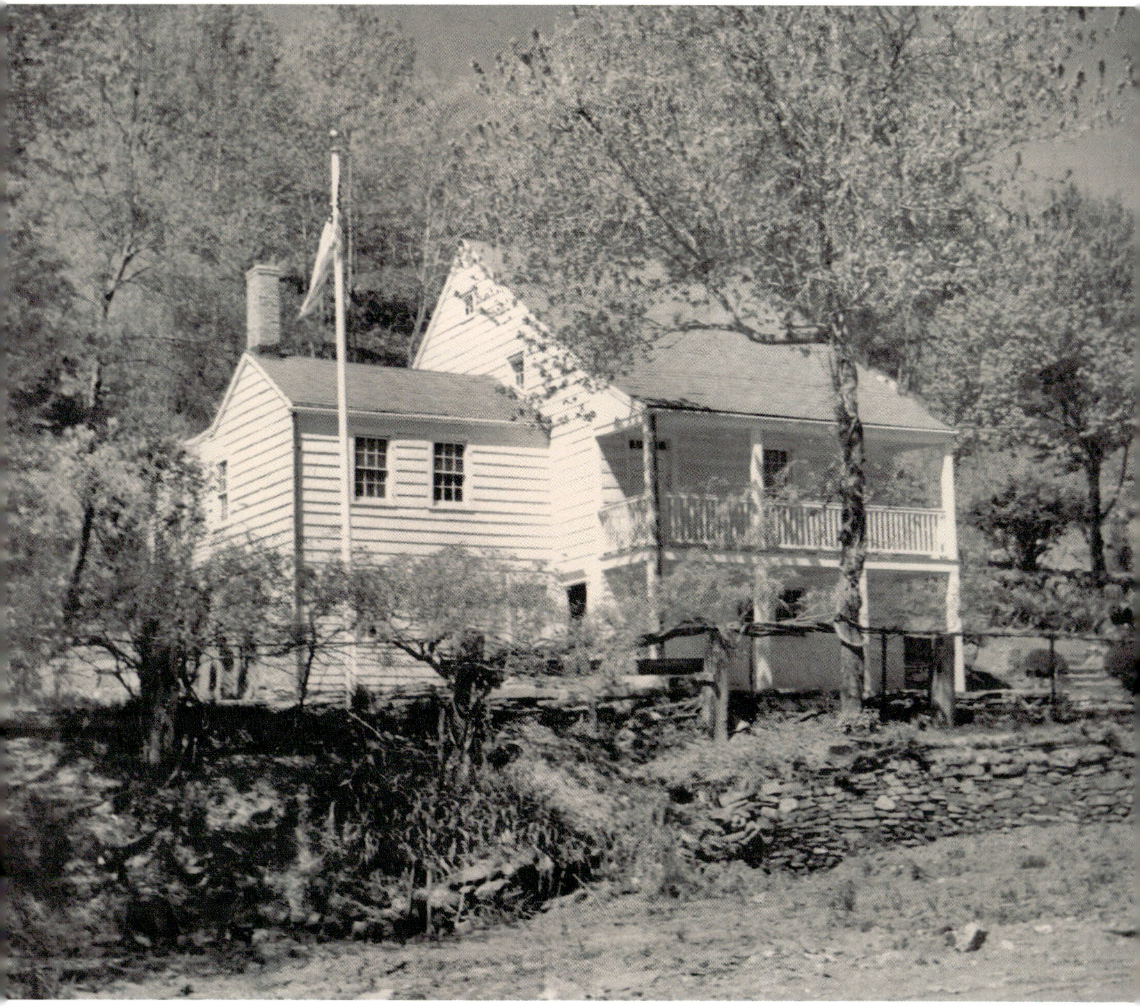

The Sherwood house was built by Stephen Sherwood, a tenant farmer of the Philipse Manor and an ensign of militia during the Revolutionary War. It became the home of John Ingersoll, Yonkers's first physician. In 1955, the Sherwood house became the property of the Yonkers Historical Society. The house is listed on the National Register of Historic Places and is a local landmark. (Courtesy of Yonkers Historical Society.)

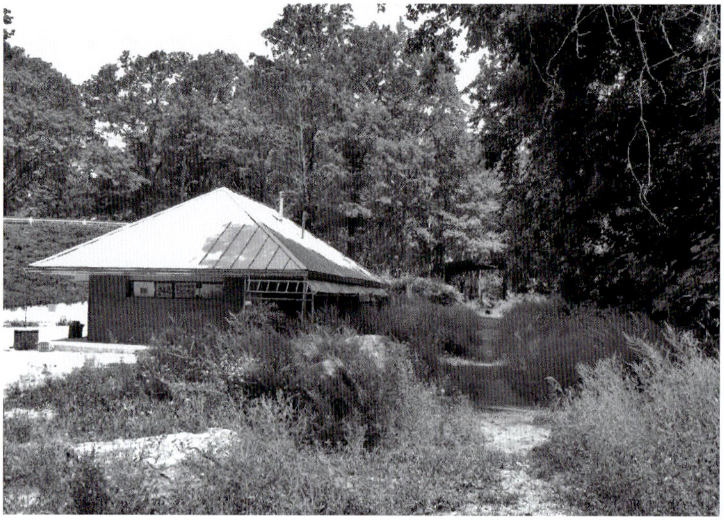

The name Bryn Mawr is a Welsh phrase that means "great hill." The stop at Bryn Mawr, located along the old Put line, is at the highest elevation of its track. The station built for this stop was one of the more elaborate along the line, featuring a stone exterior, slate roof, and scrolled rafter tails. The last lower Put freight train made its final run in August 1982. In the 1990s, a replica of the Bryn Mawr park station building was built on the site of the original building. (Courtesy of Yonkers Historical Society.)

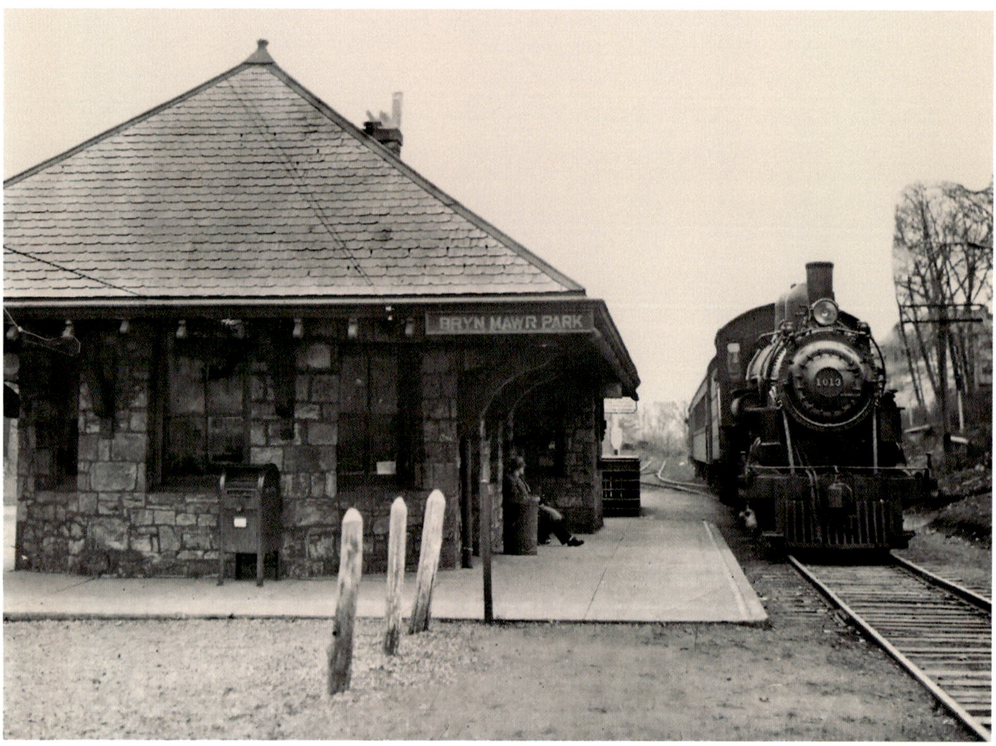

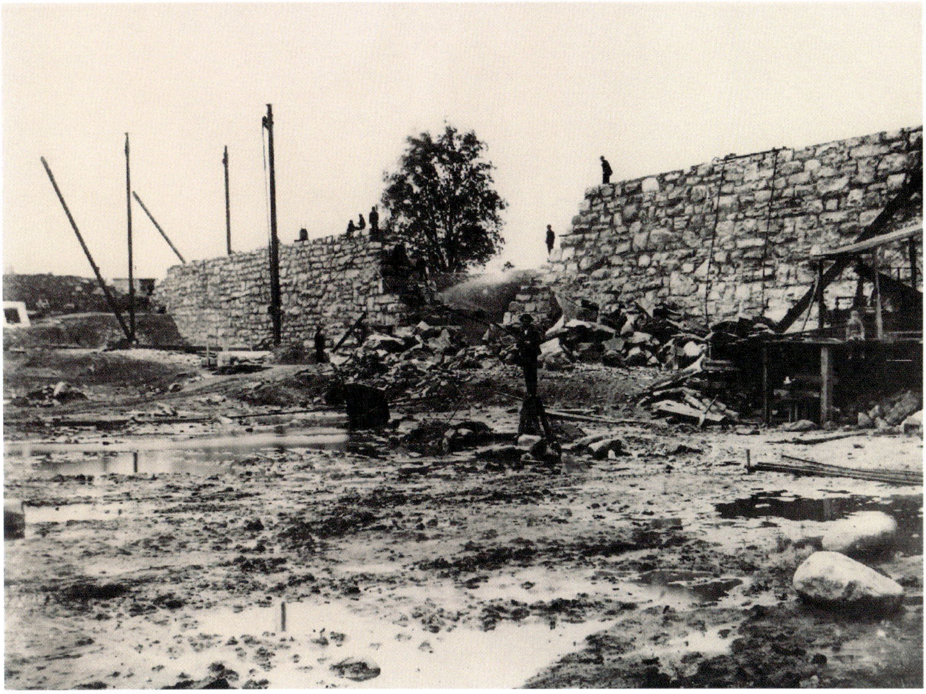

The Fortfield Reservoir was located on Palmer Road just east of the Saw Mill River Parkway. By the late 1960s, the reservoir had been drained with the site becoming the location of the Yonkers Board of Education and John Burroughs Junior High School. Today the area of the former Fortfield Reservoir is the campus of the Saunders Trades and Technical High School, which moved to the site from downtown Yonkers in 1980. (Courtesy of Hon. Nicholas Spano.)

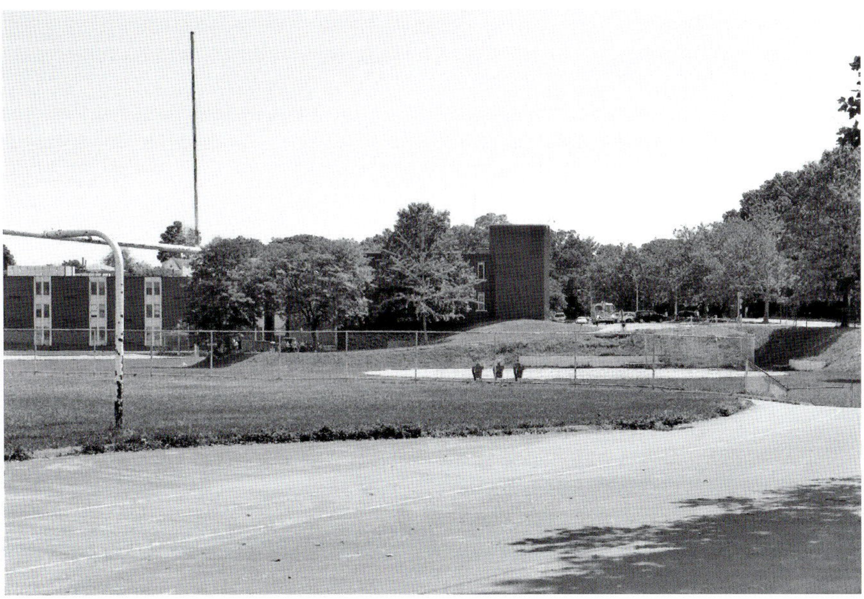

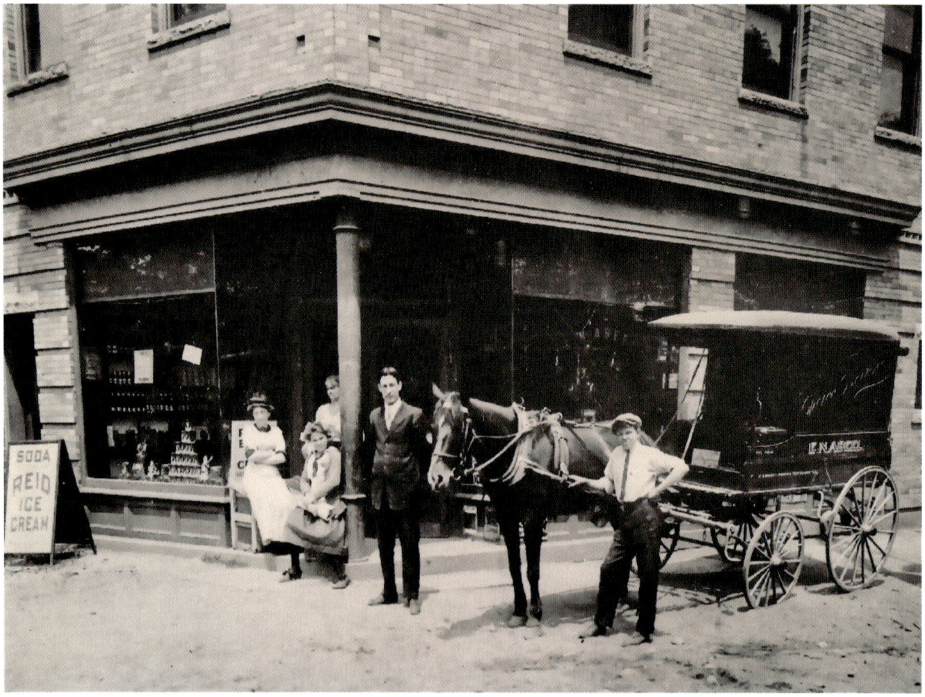

Yonkers was part of the neutral ground during the American Revolution, and both the British troops and their Hessian allies were known to have been active in the area near the junction of the Saw Mill River Road and Tuckahoe Road. Early in the 19th century, Lemuel C. Wells built Yonkers's District School No. 1 at the intersection of Saw Mill River Road and Tuckahoe Road. A blacksmith shop and a cider mill were near enough to the school for the children to watch the work and enjoy the refreshing beverage in their free time. Early in the 20th century, the historic African American community of Runyon Heights was established not far from this site. (Courtesy of Hudson River Museum.)

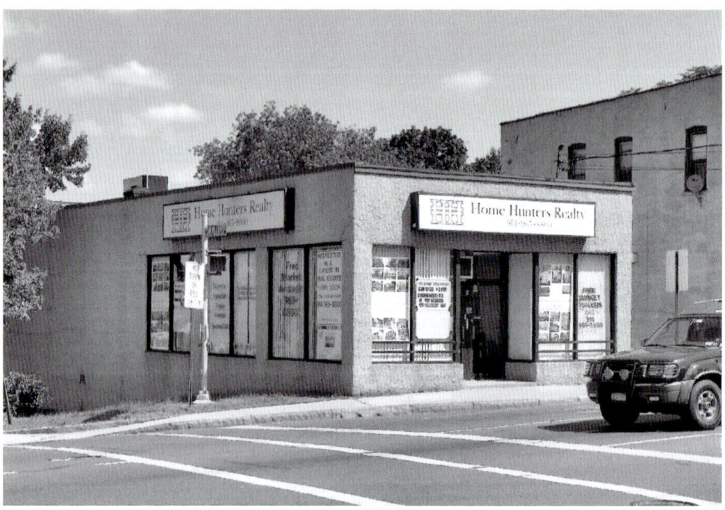

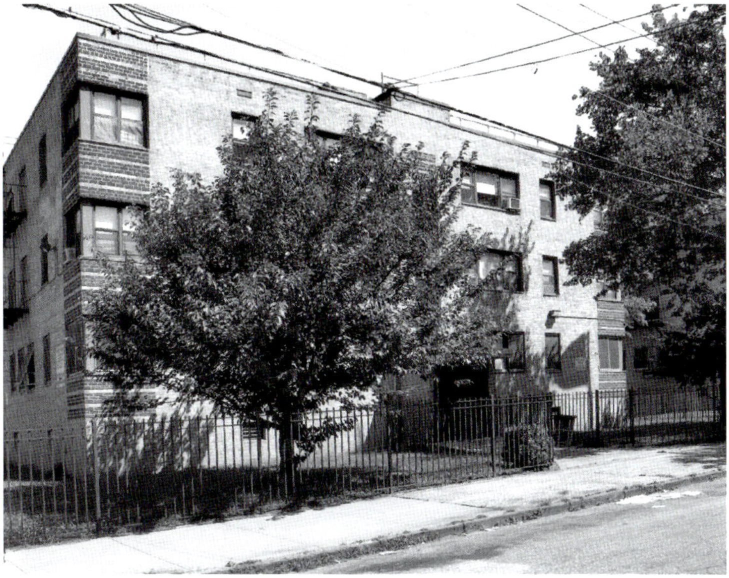

In 1876, a brick school was erected on property originally owned by Charles Runyon between Second and Third Streets on Saw Mill River Road. This school replaced the District School No. 1 on Saw Mill River Road and Tuckahoe Road and was called Public School No. 1. The building was later enlarged and stuccoed. The apartment buildings currently located on the property were built by the Yonkers Municipal Housing Authority and were first occupied in 1962. (Courtesy of Westchester County Historical Society.)

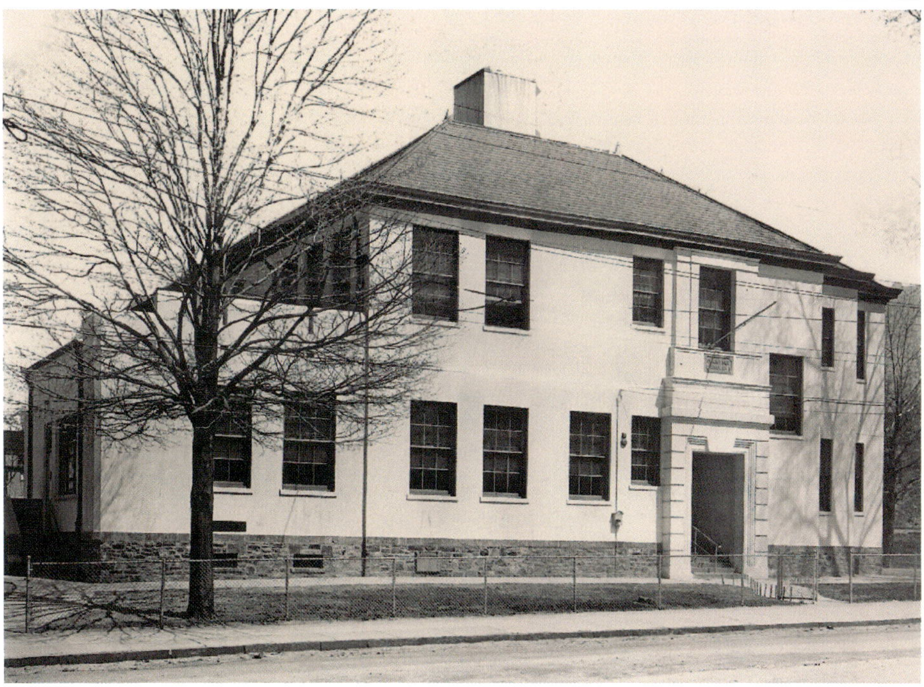

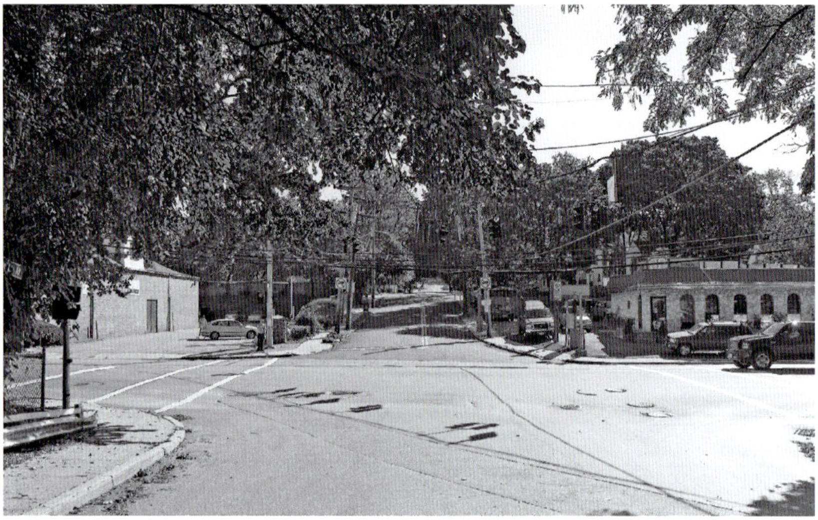

Foreseeing the growth and future of Yonkers, William B. Rice, a prosperous New England shoe manufacturer, purchased several hundred acres of valuable meadow and woodland lying directly in residential development. An advertisement in the *Time and Tribune* edition from July 12, 1925, stated, "Homefield is vastly more than a suburban development; it is a carefully planned community in every step of the way from the selection of the property itself, the laying out of the streets and avenues." (Courtesy of Yonkers Historical Society.)

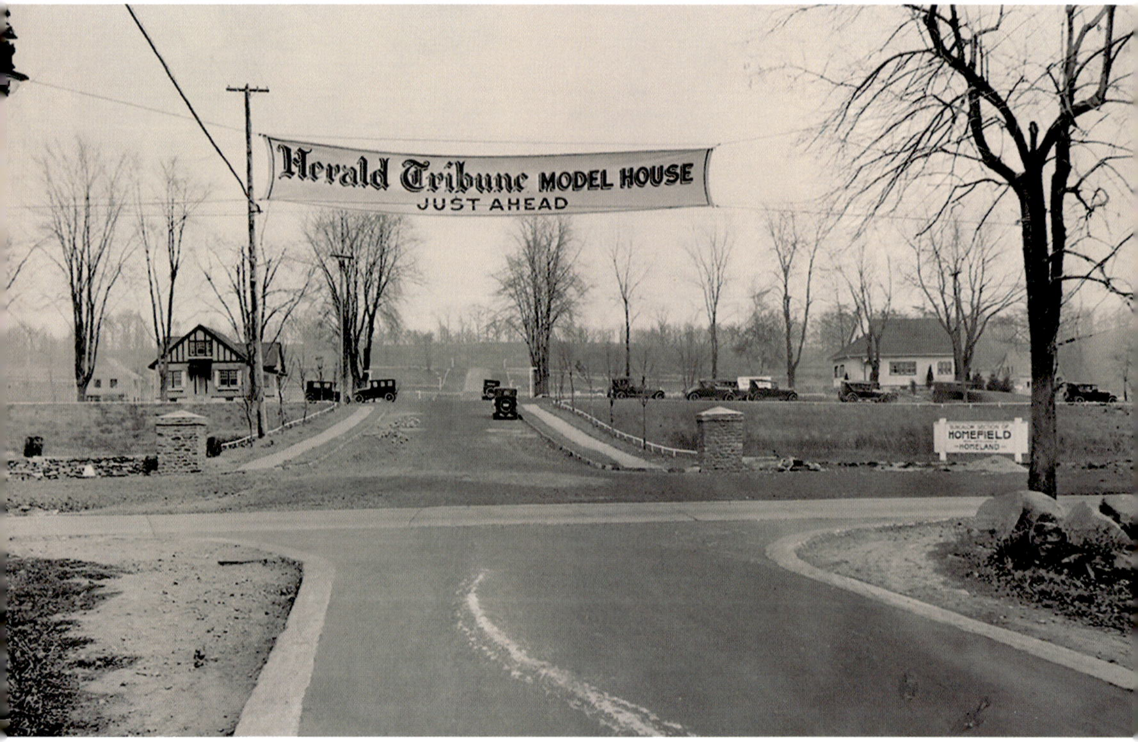

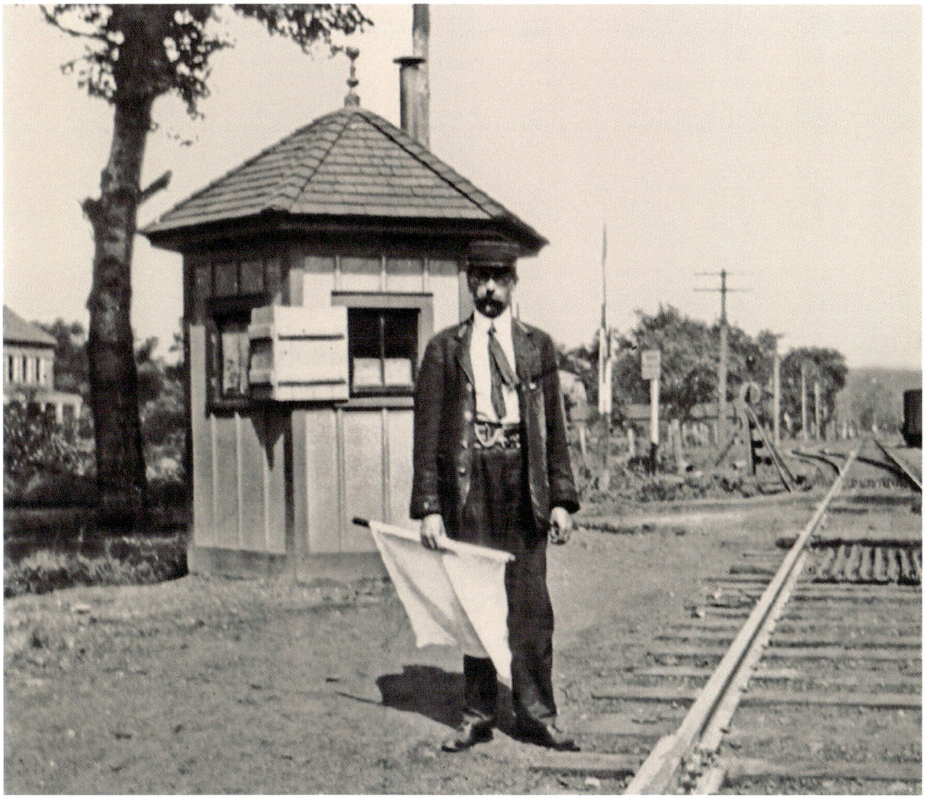

Gray Oaks train station was located at the intersection of Saw Mill River Road and Odell Avenue. The stop's only traveler amenities consisted of a covered platform. Gray Oaks was also partially used as a flag stop. At certain times of the day, waiting passengers at the station would signal or flag down the train motorman so the locomotive could be slowed in order to stop at the station. (Courtesy of Yonkers Historical Society.)

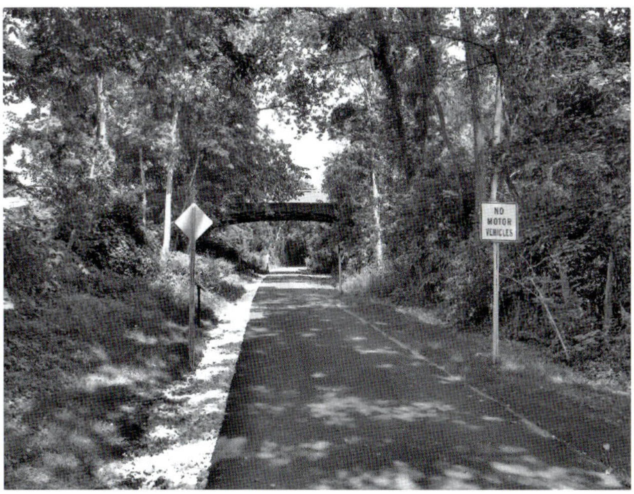

As the Bronx River Parkway opened in 1925 and the New York Central Railroad expanded service, Crestwood became an even more prestigious destination for city dwellers seeking a home in the bucolic country. This signpost, at the southern entrance to the community, proudly announced to newcomers that they had "arrived." The original sign has been lost to posterity but the welcome mat to Crestwood is always out. It is an established Yonkers community with a new public school, churches of several denominations, its own public library, and an active historical society. (Courtesy of Crestwood Historical Society.)

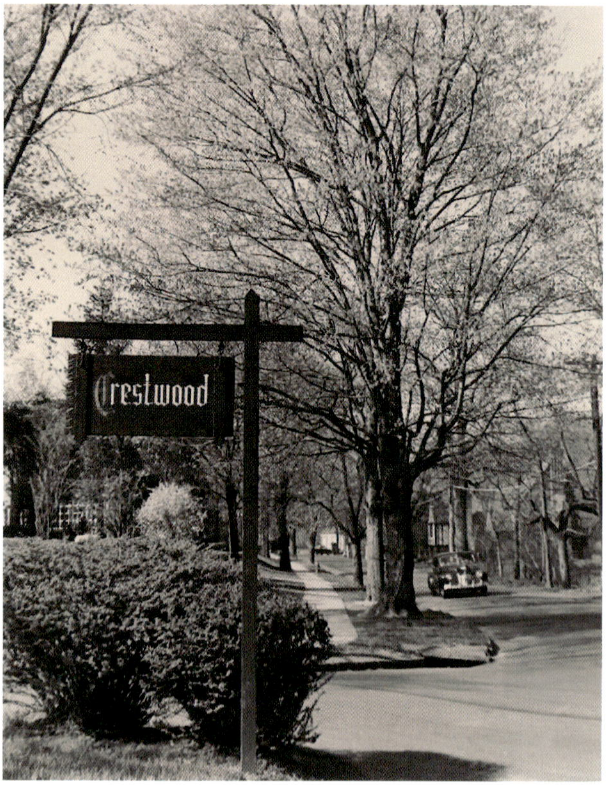

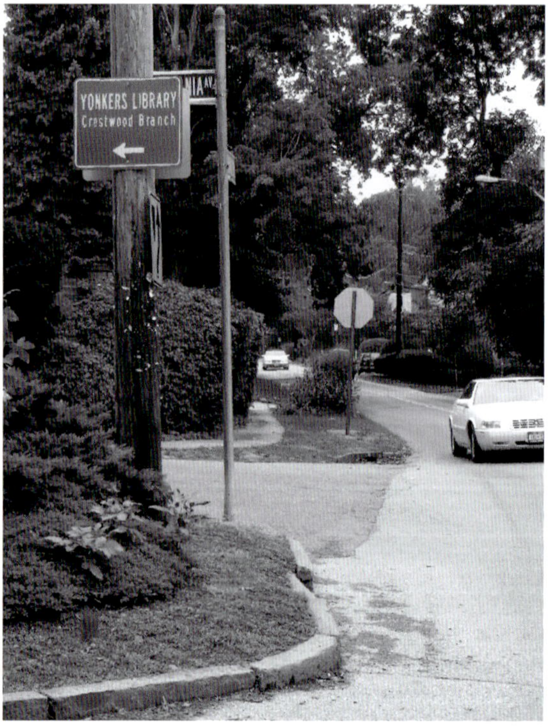

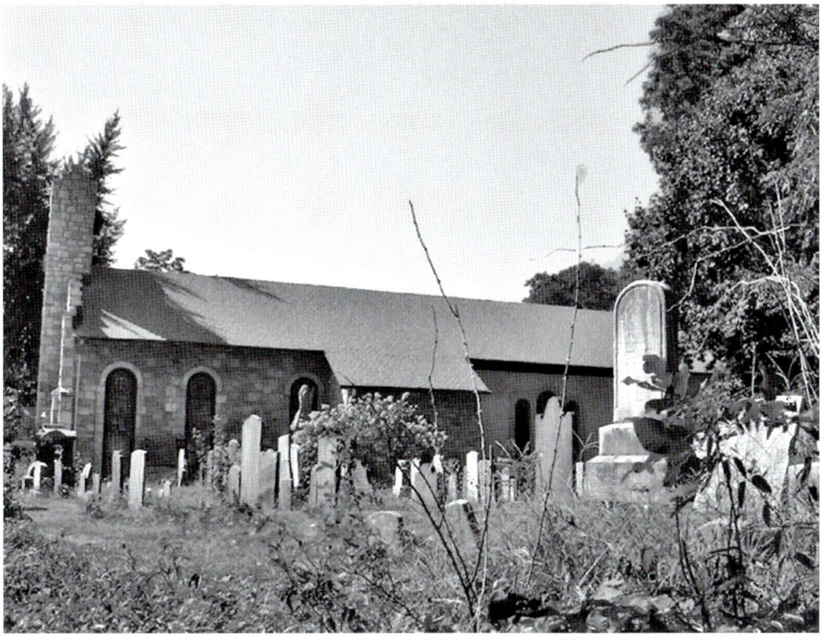

The Asbury Methodist church began as the Sherwood chapel in 1797. Silas Crawford constructed the chapel, which still stands today. The larger church replaced it in 1866. Adjacent to the church is the old burial ground, which contains the remains of most of the community pioneers. The oldest stone bears the date of 1800. In 1855, the church incorporated as the First Methodist Episcopal Church of Yonkers, a corporate name it retained until 1942 when it was changed to the Asbury Methodist Church of Crestwood, New York. (Courtesy of Crestwood Historical Society.)

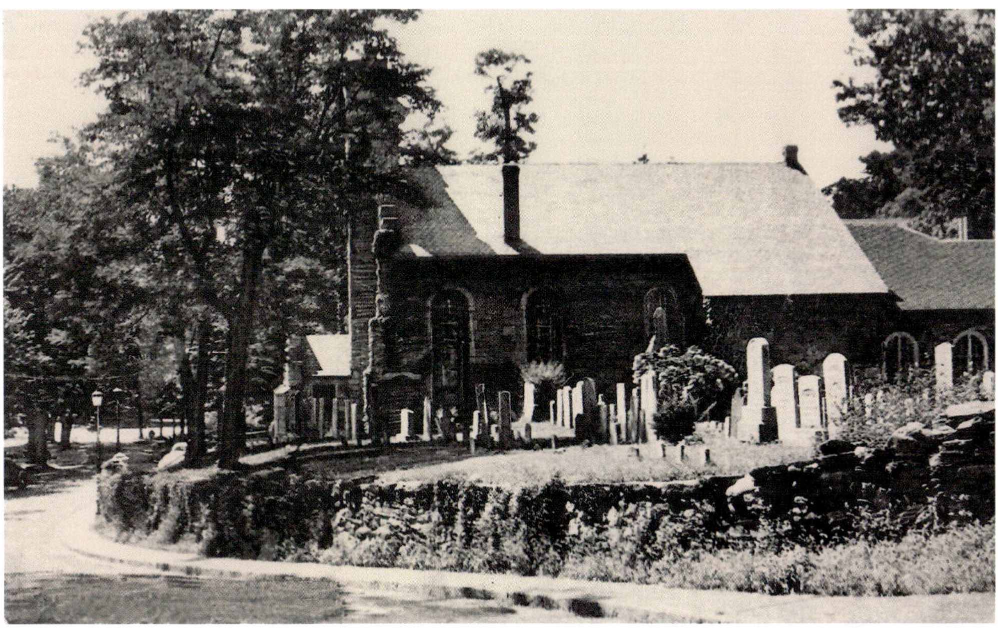

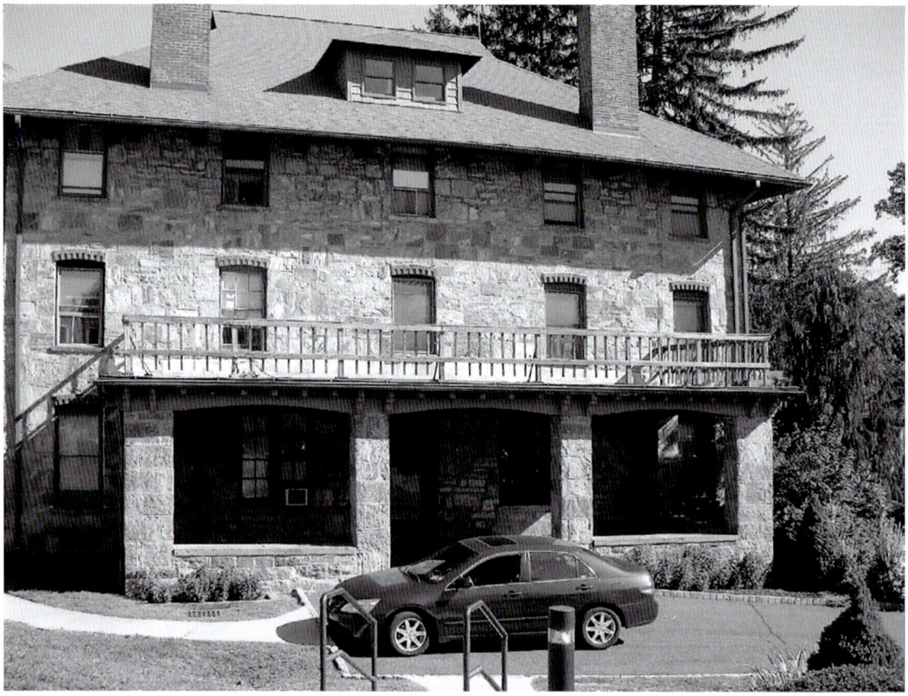

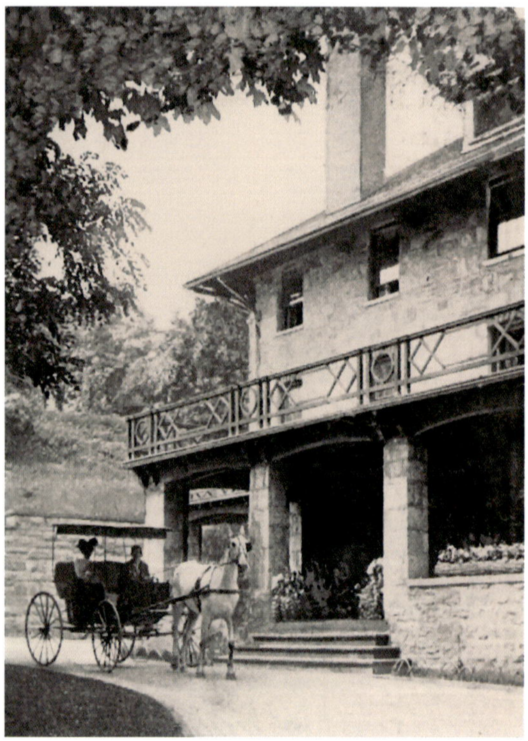

On land originally owned by the loyalist Philipse family during the Revolutionary War, the Iselin family's farm became the site of the new nation's first free convalescent home. Operated by the Sisters of Charity, the home provided restorative care for invalids and convalescing new mothers and their children. The home opened in 1901 and was completely financed by the generous Iselin family. There were 33 rooms where 10 nuns cared for 40 women and 20 children until 1961, when the Roman Catholic order sold the grounds to St. Vladimir's Seminary. (Courtesy of Crestwood Historical Society.)

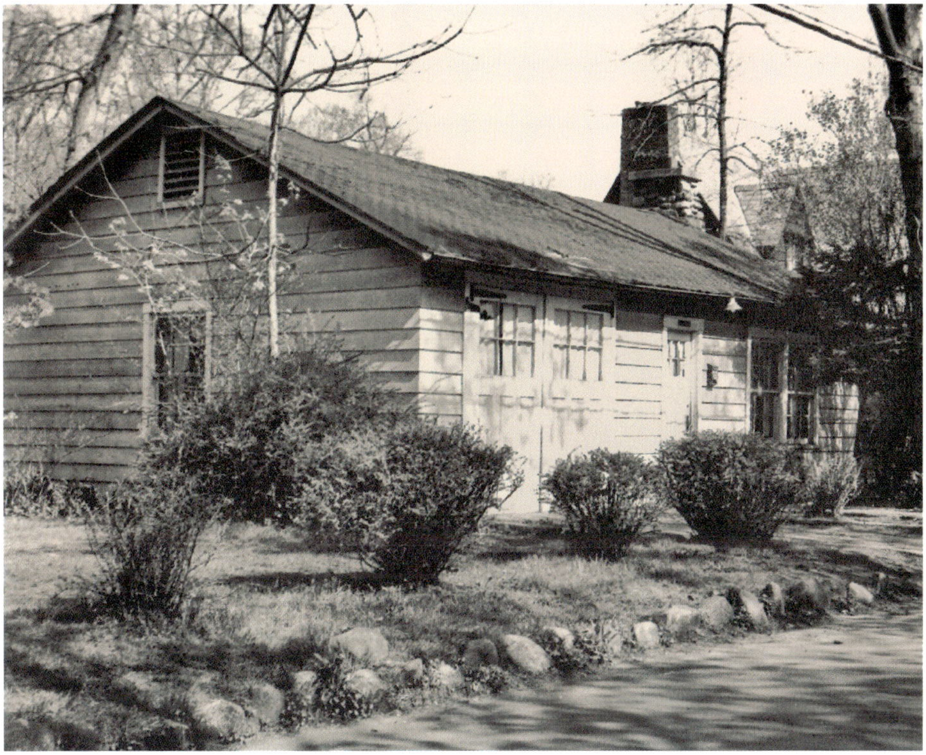

The Crestwood Chemical Engine and Hose Company was founded in 1902 with 10 volunteers. The company was originally located in a barn near School 15. Crestwood residents purchased the pump and wagon and offered the growing company larger quarters at another location, until several years later when the volunteers built themselves this house, which is still standing at 187 Scarsdale Road at the intersection with Pennsylvania Avenue. In its present incarnation, it has been converted into a private home with a bright red door. (Courtesy of Crestwood Historical Society.)

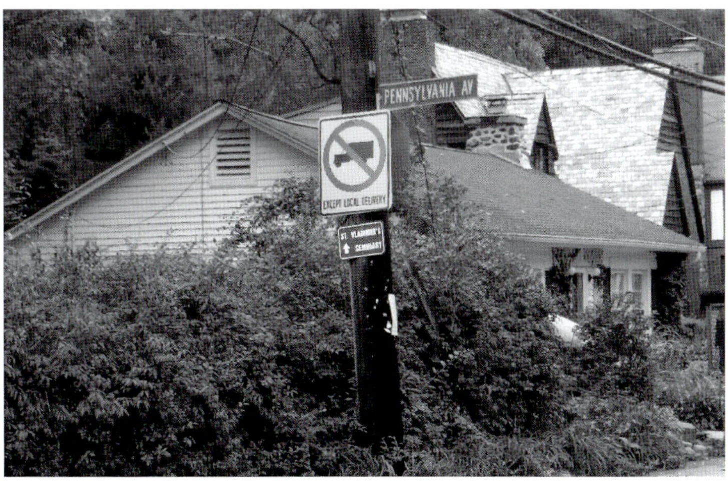

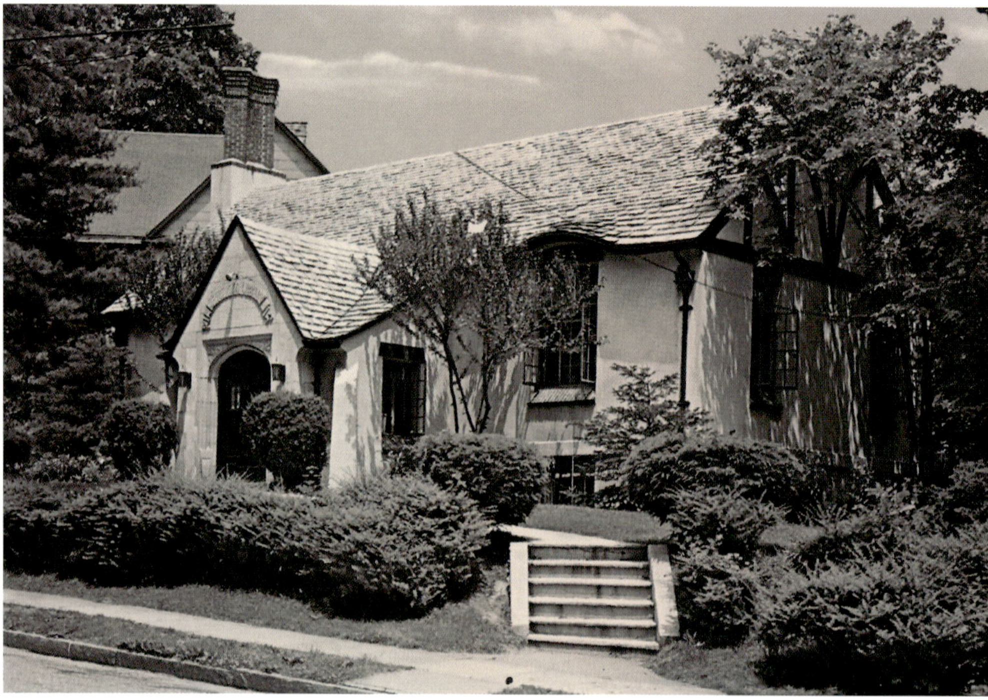

Shortly after World War I, the Crestwood Women's Club acquired the land where this building now stands on Thompson Street. The property was donated to the City of Yonkers with the written understanding that a library would be built on the site. When city finances faltered, it fell to the community to complete construction, and local fund-raising drives raised enough to finish the exterior and roof. In 1926, with the bookshelves stocked, the library opened and ultimately became a branch of the Yonkers Public Library system. (Courtesy of Crestwood Historical Society.)

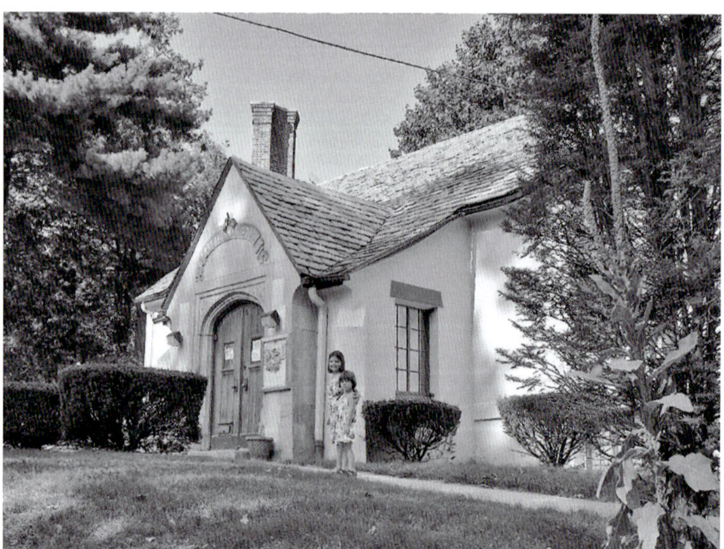

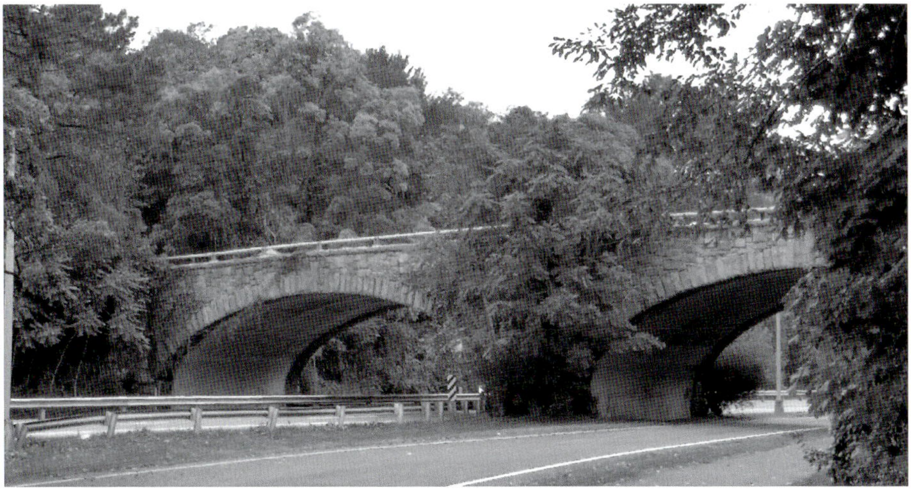

The Crestwood community celebrated the 75th anniversary of the opening of the Bronx River Parkway in October 2000. The parkway was a cooperative effort between Westchester County and New York City and is the first limited-access parkway in the United States. The Bronx River and the parkway had an enormous impact on the development of Crestwood. Originally part of a Dutch land grant to the Philipse family that extended from the Hudson River to the Bronx River, Crestwood was mostly comprised of 125 acres purchased by Abigail Sherwood under the acts of dissolution in 1786. (Courtesy of Crestwood Historical Society.)

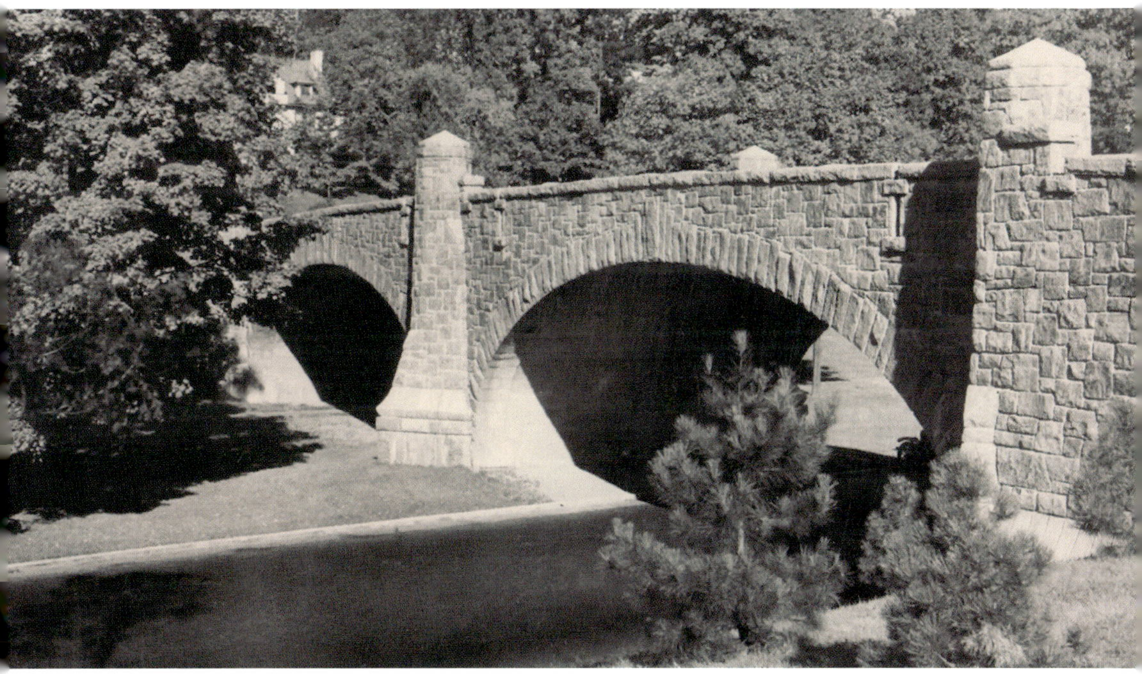

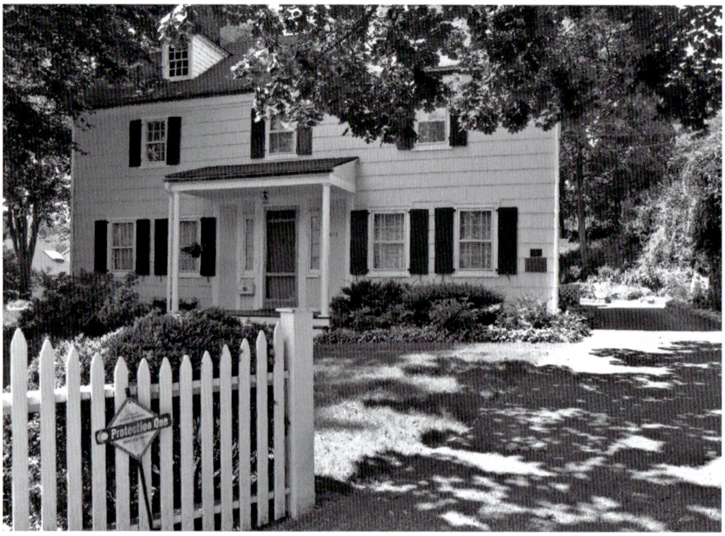

The oldest private residence in Yonkers, the original part of Hart House on Bronxville Road was erected about 1760 by Eleazer Hart, a tenant farmer of Philipse Manor. The front portion of the house was built in 1780. The early portion of the house, with its Dutch oven and smoke house, is in the rear. The house has been remodeled, but the original house is still recognizable. The owners have retained many of its older parts and obtained local landmark designation for the site. Preservation laws have guaranteed its enduring example of Yonkers's link to its Colonial past. (Courtesy of Yonkers Historical Society.)

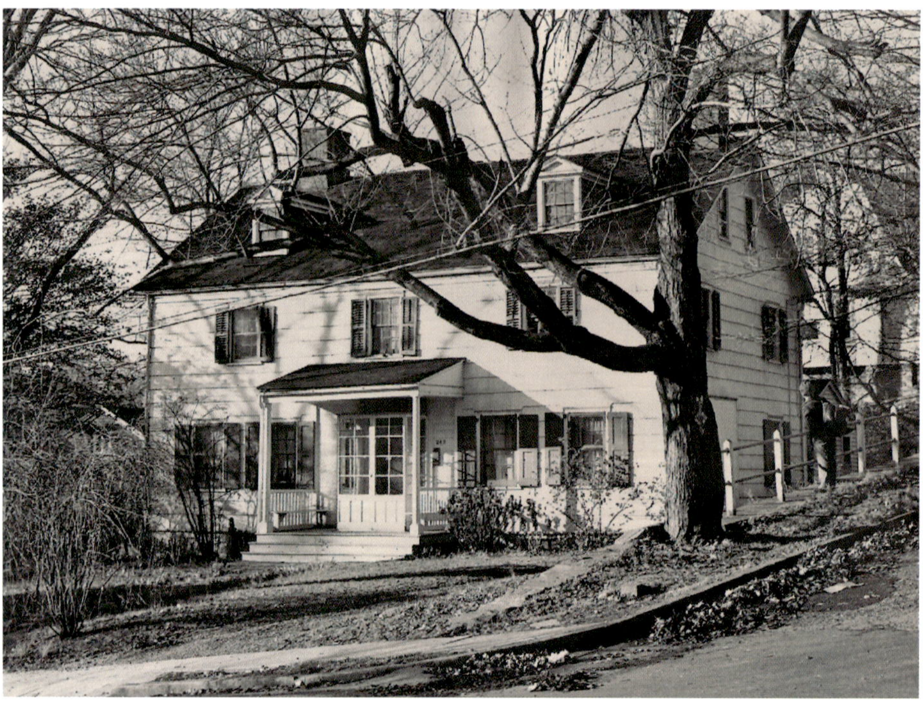

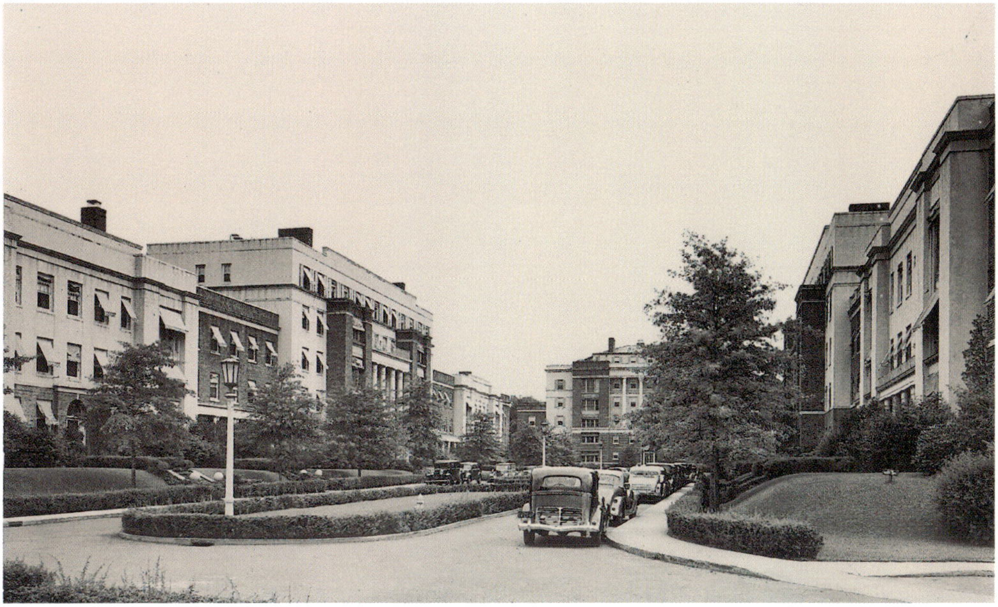

Winding, narrow roads contribute to both the parklike charm and the privacy of a wealthy enclave on the eastern edge of Yonkers known as Lawrence Park West. The area is the home of Sarah Lawrence College, beautiful estates, and some apartment houses, one of which is Brookland Gardens. Many people think of Lawrence Park West as part of Bronxville instead of Yonkers. To add to the confusion, its post office designation is Bronxville. (Courtesy of Yonkers Planning Bureau.)

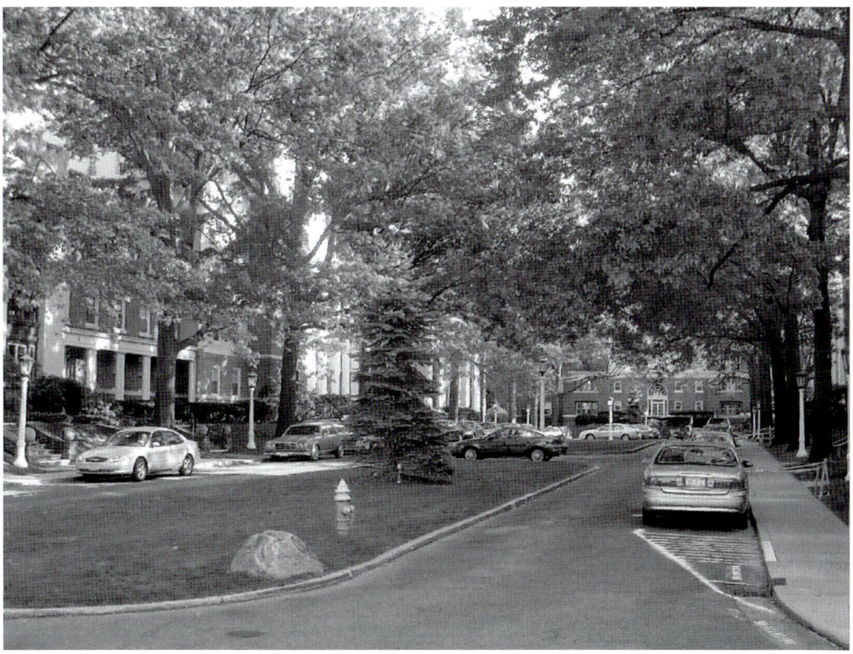

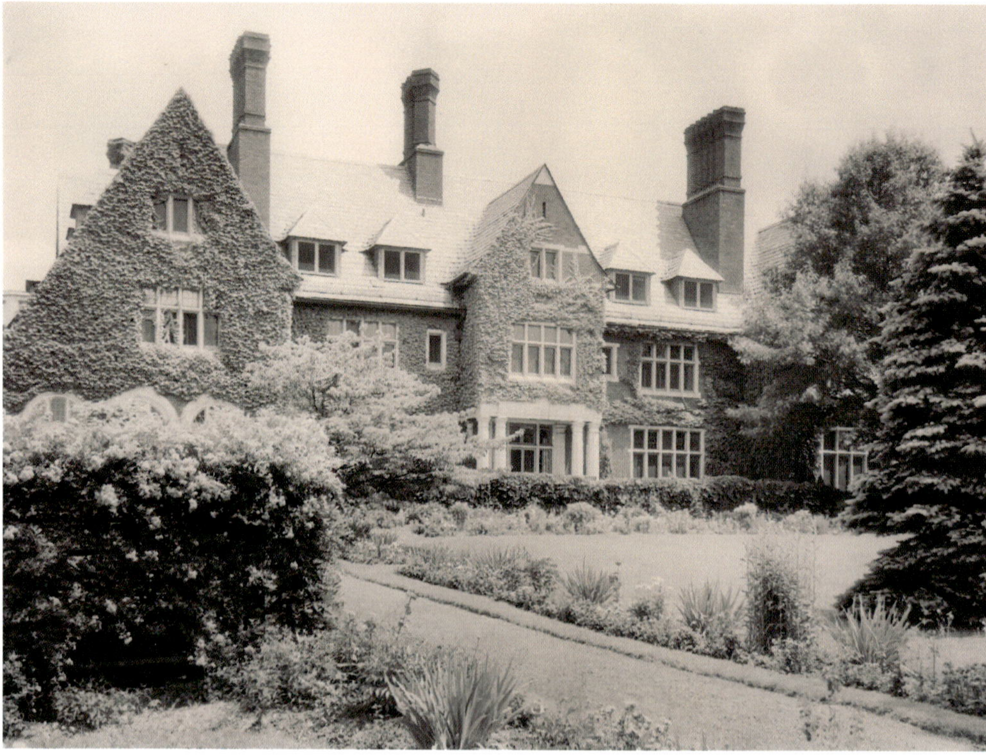

Choosing Lawrence Park West for his home in 1914, William Van Duzer Lawrence built a majestic stone house and named it Westlands. The building is now the administration building of Sarah Lawrence College. The college was a memorial for his wife, Sarah, and he considered this the most fitting tribute to her great interest in higher education. The college opened in 1928. (Courtesy of Yonkers Historical Society.)

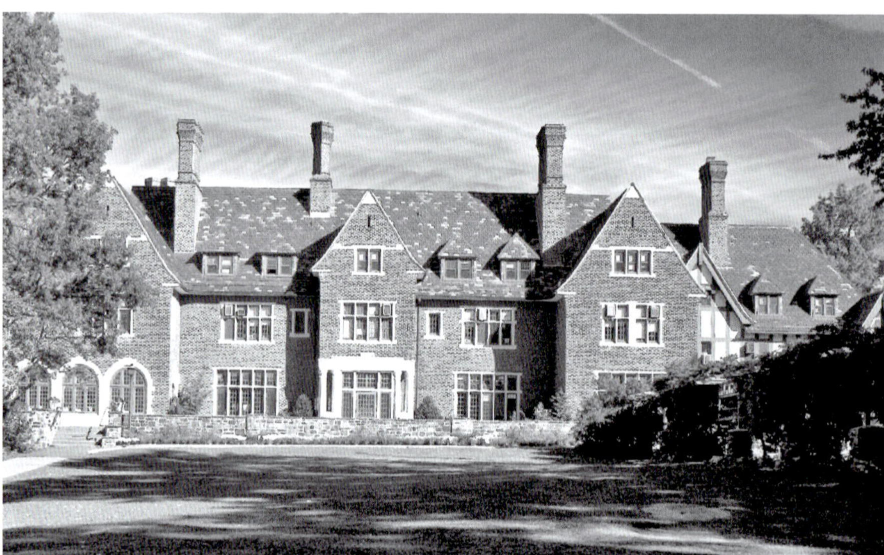

CHAPTER

SOUTHEAST YONKERS

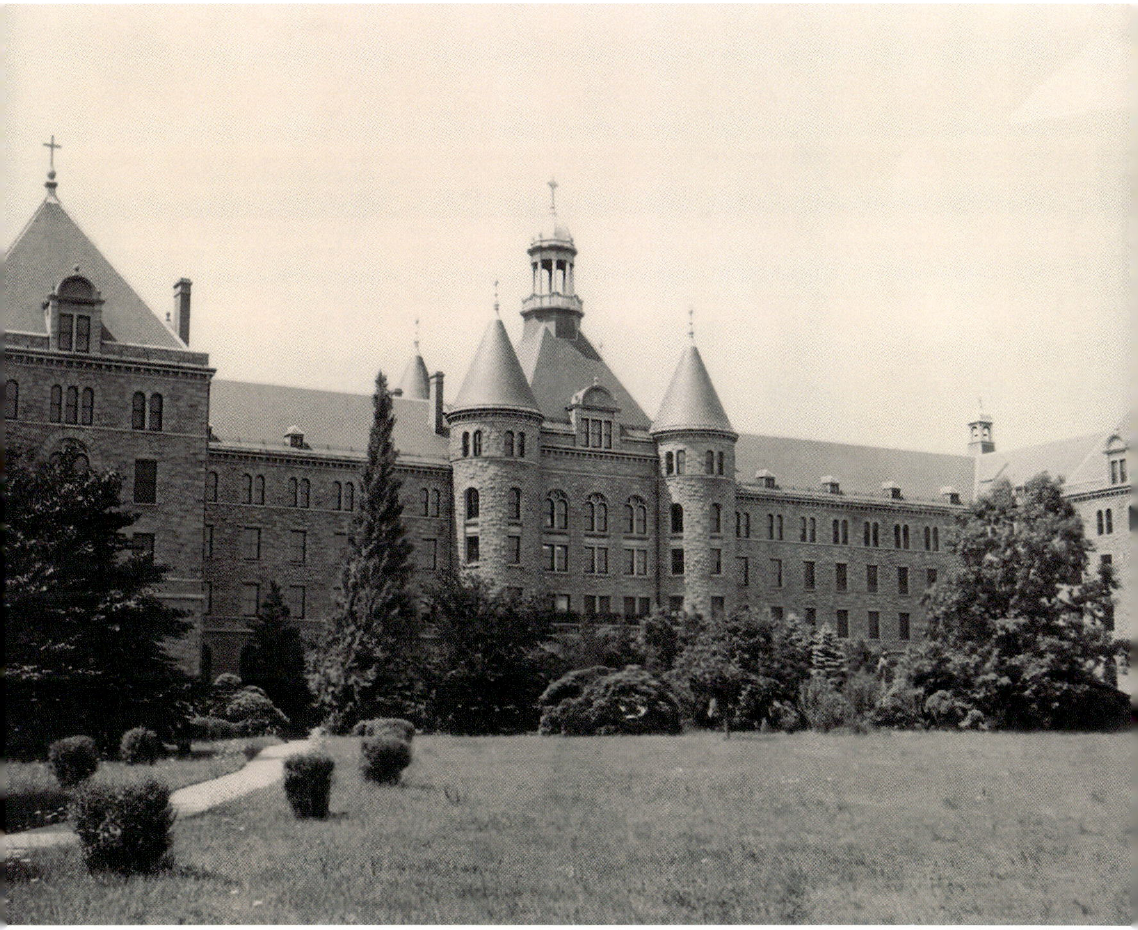

Situated atop historic Valentine Hill where George Washington briefly had headquarters in October 1776, St. Joseph's Seminary has been educating men for the priesthood since 1896. More than 40,000 people are said to have been present on Pentecost Sunday 1891, when Archbishop Michael Corrigan blessed the cornerstone. Visiting cardinals have traditionally planted a tree on the seminary grounds. Pope John Paul II visited the seminary in October 1995. (Courtesy of Yonkers Historical Society.)

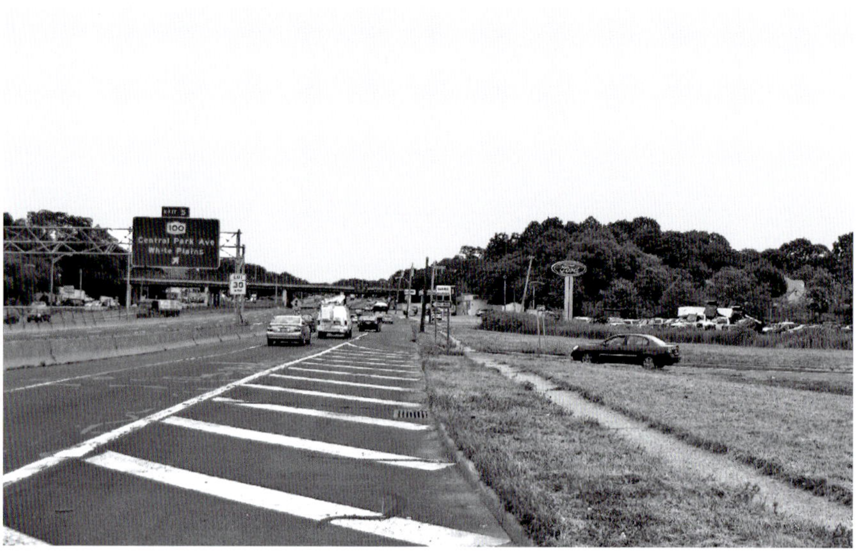

The development of Central Park Avenue from its beginnings some 135 years ago parallels the growth of many of the major highways in the country. Once a small avenue connecting sparsely populated rural areas, today Central Park Avenue is a major thoroughfare that has evolved into a major shopping (Cross County Center) and an entertainment area that serves residents of Westchester and thousands of visitors a day from nearby areas. (Courtesy of Yonkers Historical Society.)

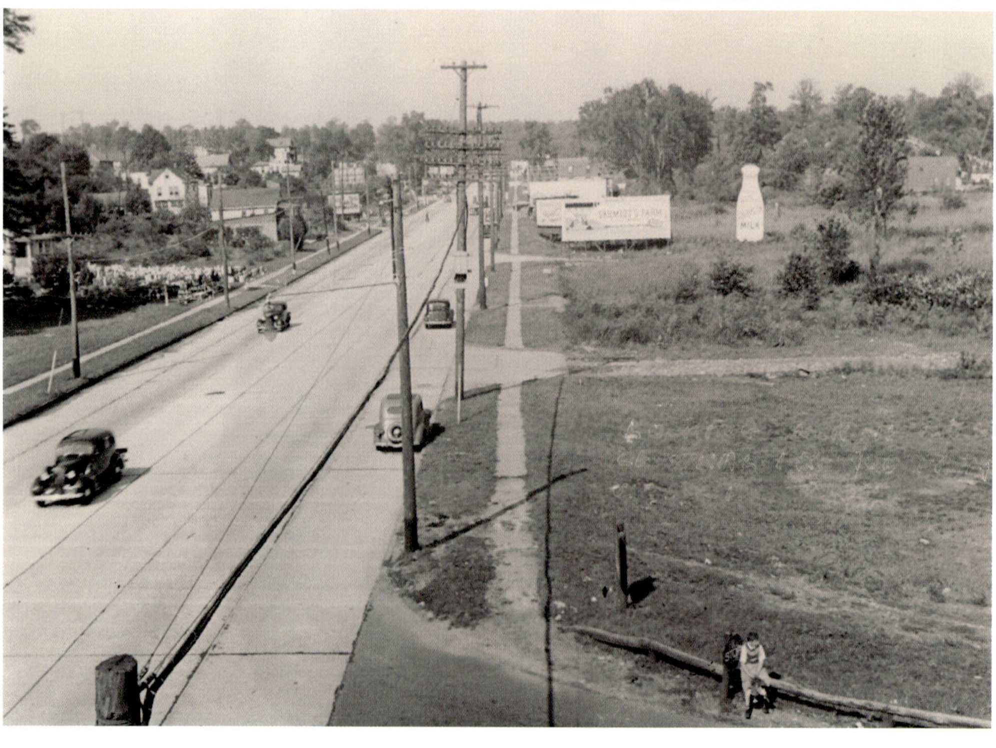

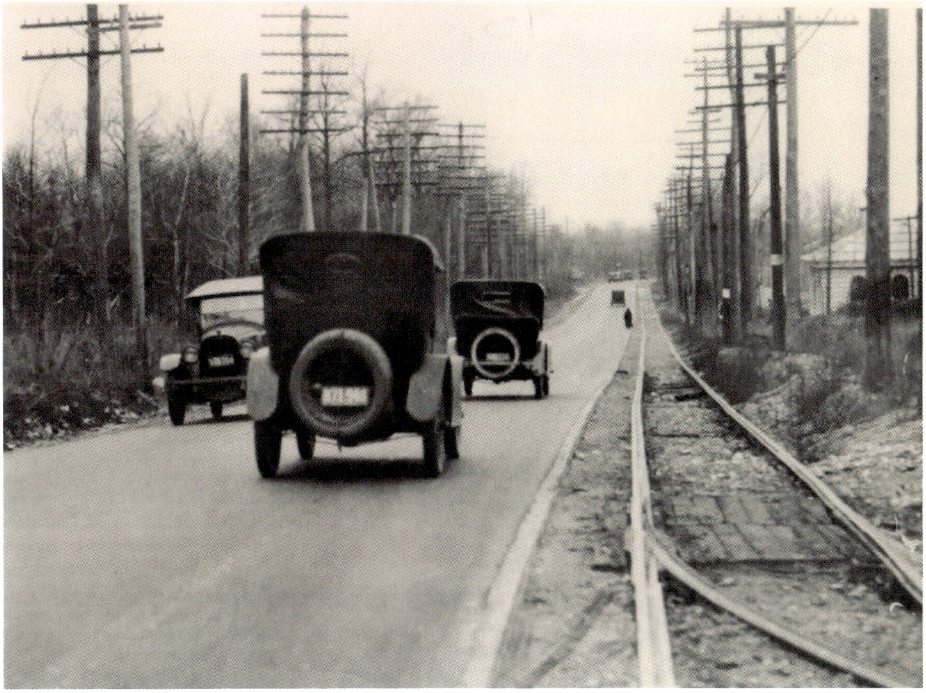

McLean Avenue is named for the late Maj. George W. McLean, who for 20 years resided at Highland. He bought the property as a country estate in 1884. He was one of the most prominent citizens of this time, having been president of the New York Stock Exchange. The mansion was razed in 1907 for the Hillview Reservoir. The historic photograph shows Central Avenue adjacent to the property. (Courtesy of Donald Kreutzberg.)

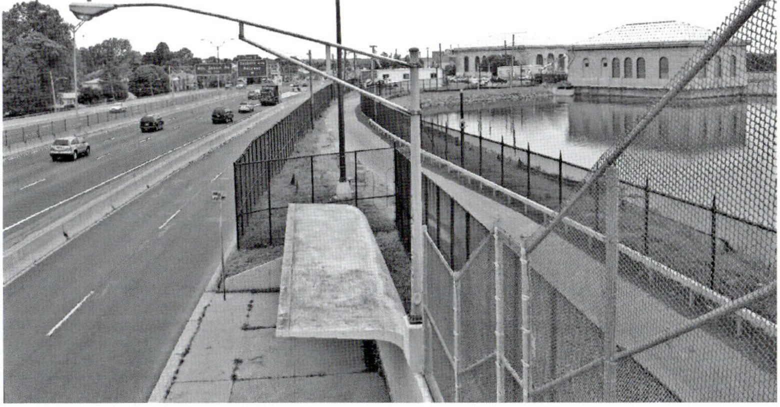

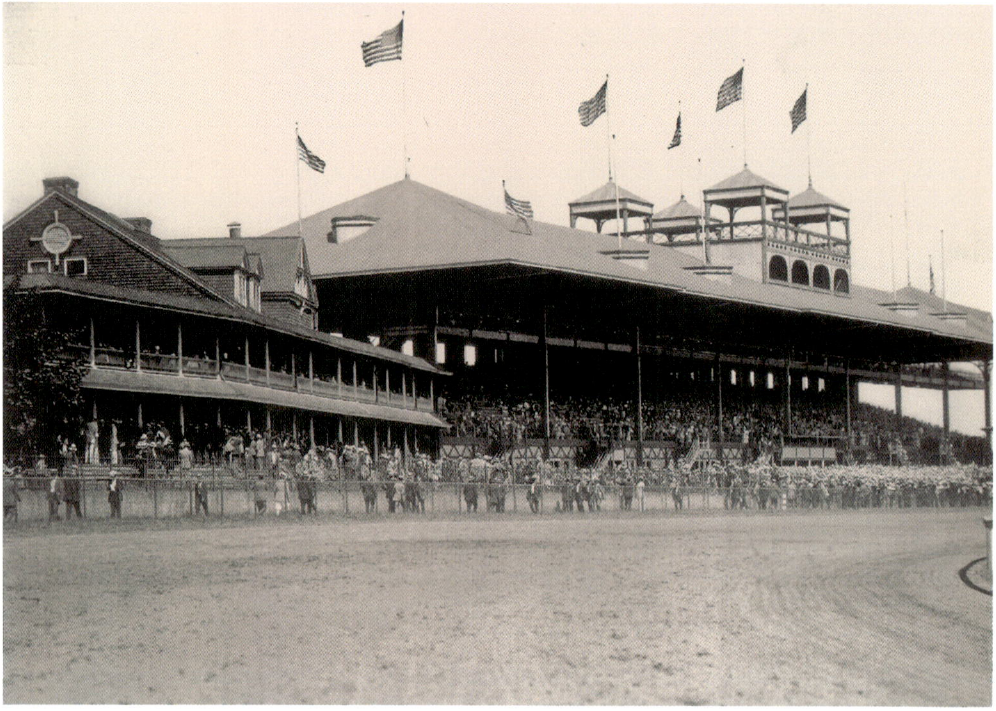

Empire City Racetrack opened on Labor Day 1899 as a harness racing track on the present site of the Yonkers Raceway. Some of America's best jockeys performed regularly at Empire City Racetrack. In 1950, the facility was renovated and reopened as the Yonkers Raceway. The racetrack was then bought by the Rooney family in 1972. In 2004, Yonkers Raceway began a major renovation project, installing video lottery terminals to supplement its live harness racing. In October 2006, Empire City at Yonkers Raceway opened with video slot machines. (Courtesy of Yonkers Raceway.)

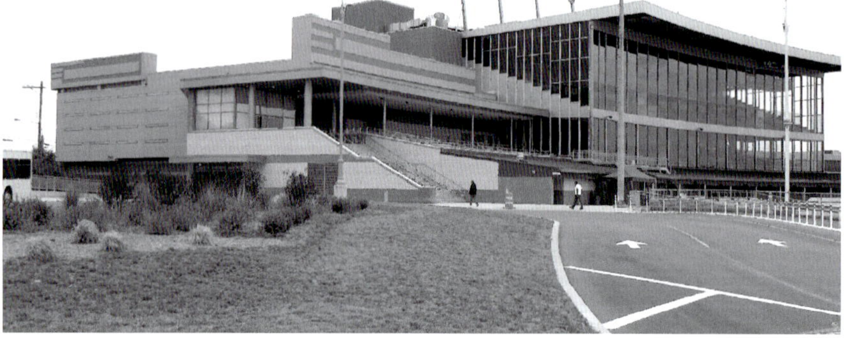

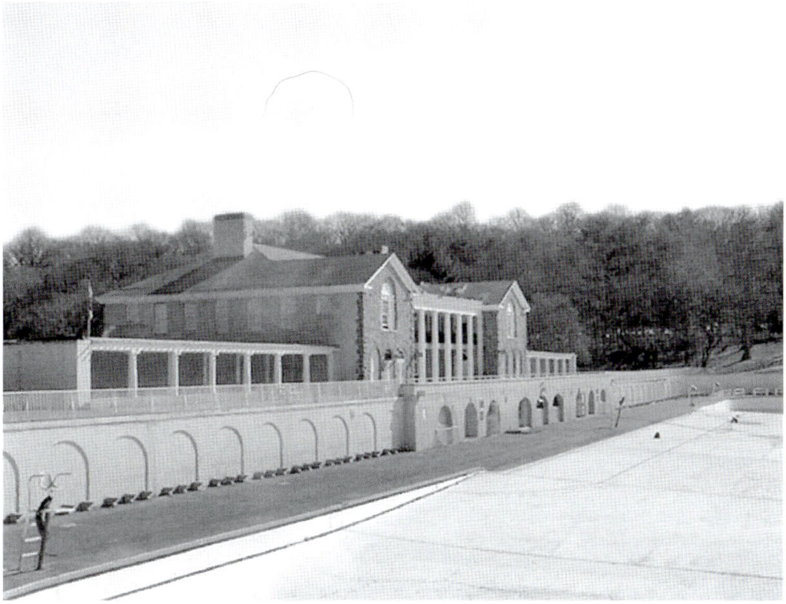

In the 1920s, the Tibbetts Brook Valley, with its well wooded, rocky slopes was identified as the location of a county park to be developed by the newly formed Westchester County Park Commission. Tibbetts Brook Park, completed in 1927, was developed on both sides of the Putnam Division right-of-way and features two lakes, a swimming facility, a bathhouse, trails, and athletic fields all connected by a series of pedestrian paths and vehicular drives. (Courtesy of Westchester County Historical Society.)

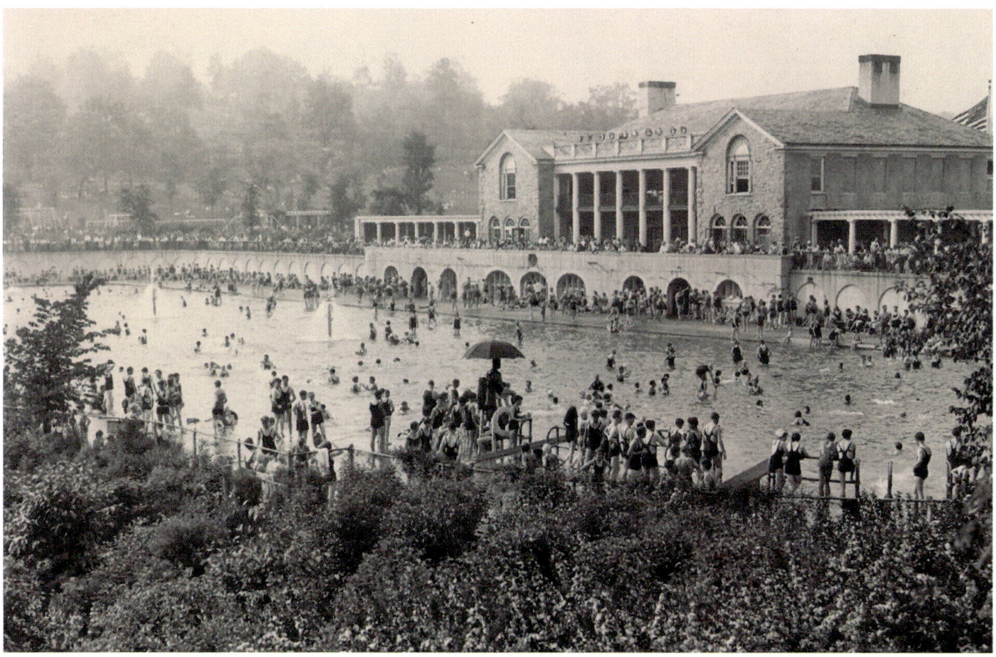